Harpers Ferry Under Fire

A Border Town in the American Civil War

Harpers Ferry Under Fire

A Border Town in the American Civil War

DENNIS E. FRYE
Chief Historian
Harpers Ferry National Historical Park

Harpers Ferry Historical Association
P.O. Box 197
Harpers Ferry, WV 25425
304-535-6881
hfha@earthlink.net
www.harpersferryhistory.org

THE
DONNING COMPANY
PUBLISHERS

Catherine Baldau, *Project Manager*

The Harpers Ferry Historical Association is a nonprofit cooperating association supporting the education and interpretive programs of Harpers Ferry National Historical Park. All proceeds from the sale of this publication benefit park programs.

The Donning Company Publishers
184 Business Park Drive, Suite 206
Virginia Beach, VA 23462

Steve Mull, *General Manager*
Barbara B. Buchanan, *Office Manager*
Richard A. Horwege, *Senior Editor*
Stephanie Danko, *Graphic Designer*
Priscilla Odango, *Imaging Artist*
Lori Porter, *Project Research Coordinator*
Tonya Washam, *Marketing Specialist*
Pamela Engelhard, *Marketing Advisor*

Dennis N. Walton, *Project Director*

Library of Congress Cataloging-in-Publication Data

Frye, Dennis E.
      Harpers Ferry under fire : a border town in the American Civil War /
Dennis E. Frye.
            p.   cm.
      Includes bibliographical references and index.
      ISBN 978-1-57864-716-3 (soft cover : alk. paper)
      ISBN 978-1-57864-751-4 (hard cover : alk. paper)
      1. Harpers Ferry (W. Va.)—History—19th century. 2. West Virginia—
History—Civil War, 1861–1865. I. Title.
      F249.H2F79 2011
      975.4'99—dc23
                                                                              2011042699
Printed in the USA at Walsworth Publishing Company

This book is dedicated to Superintendent Donald W. Campbell, who tirelessly worked for three decades to preserve and protect the Harpers Ferry Battlefield.

And to Debbie Piscitelli, whose contributions and commitment to the interpretation and education programs at Harpers Ferry enabled flourishment throughout her three decades of leadership of the Harpers Ferry Historical Association.

Acknowledgments

This book has been years in making, and many people are responsible for its contents.

Park Superintendent Don Campbell and Chief of Interpretation Paul Lee supported and permitted my scholarly research at institutions across the country. Park Superintendent Rebecca Harriett granted me the opportunity to prepare the manuscript for the interpretation and education staffs that ultimately transitioned into this illustrated volume. Curators Hilda Staubs and Michelle Hammer generously assisted with my hours of probing into the Harpers Ferry Park collection. Ranger Supervisors Paul Lee, Todd Bolton, John King, and Catherine Bragaw helped inspire me with their wisdom and insights. Interpretive Specialist Marsha Wassel contributed her photography skills, and Historian Rangers Richard Gillespie, David Larsen, Jeff Bowers, John Powell, Melinda Day, David Fox, and Jim Ogden eagerly shared their multitude of discoveries. Park Architect Peter Dessauer and Landscape Architect Steve Lowe have been passionate supporters of my efforts. Thanks are also extended to Susan Haberkorn for her assistance in preparing and reviewing the manuscript.

Speaking of discoveries, treasures from the National Archives appear throughout this work through the selfless sharing of Michael Musick. Dr. Richard Sommers guided me through the manuscripts at the U.S. Army Military History Institute, and former NPS Chief Historian Ed Bearss always forwarded me anything concerning Harpers Ferry. Bob Krick sent me nuggets on a routine basis from his Fredericksburg headquarters, as did Ted Alexander from the Antietam archives. Dr. Bud Robertson often surprised me with jewels from his Virginia Tech repository, and Dr. Gary Gallagher kept me in mind during his research expeditions. NPS Regional Archeologist Dr. Stephen Potter has remained a study guide and inspiration. Local historians who contributed include John Divine, the sage of Loudoun County, Virginia; John Frye, the oracle of Washington County, Maryland; Ben Ritter, the encyclopedia of Frederick County, Virginia; and Dr. Millard Bushong, my mentor on Jefferson County, West Virginia.

Others who deserve special note are Gene Thorp, creator of excellent maps; and Nicolas Picerno, who gladly donated unpublished material from his vast collection.

Special acknowledgment goes to my wife, Sylvia, and my two Boston Terriers, Lincoln and Bonnie Blue, for the many hours I spent in the 19th century rather than with them.

Debbie Piscitelli and Catherine Baldau deserve five-star status for this beautiful volume. Debbie loves books! For the past 30 years, she has built and guided the Harpers Ferry Historical Association and its bookstore into a premier national park destination. Debbie's vision, persistence, and patience have provided Harpers Ferry Park with countless contributions, and Debbie's commitment to historical interpretation produced this book. Cathy spent hours transforming an in-house interpretive document into a first-class public narrative, then researching and inserting hundreds of images to illustrate the text. Cathy's careful eyes enhanced the stories revealed within.

Many labored long and hard to bring you *Harpers Ferry Under Fire*. None of our labors or hardships compared, however, to the trials and tribulations of the people in Harpers Ferry during the Civil War.

Contents

*"In future years traveler and tourist will eagerly resort [here]...
and history will point out [this] as the spot where many acts in
the great tragedy, not yet closed, took place."*

—John D. Smith, 19th Maine Infantry, September 1862

Lieutenant Roger Jones was in a quandary. Less than 24 hours ago he was on U.S. soil, charged with protecting the U.S. Armory and Arsenal, a vast Federal arms-making operation and stockpile of 15,000 weapons. Now he found himself in enemy territory, and the enemy—more than three times his size—was fast approaching.

This same town, these same arsenals, had been raided just 18 months earlier by a small band of abolitionists led by John Brown. Civilians had taken up arms; innocent townspeople were killed before local militia and a small force of U.S. Marines suppressed the raiders. Ever since, the residents had been on edge, fearful of rumored abolitionist attacks, and mistrusting of their neighbors whose mixed loyalties were exposed in the escalating secession rhetoric.

Earlier in the day, the announcement of Virginia's secession incited riots in the streets. The crowd—half feeling betrayed and half euphoric to see their state join the Confederacy—finally quieted at dusk. They returned to their homes plagued with uncertainty. What if the war came to their town? What would happen to their jobs, their livelihoods? How would they protect their families? For Lieutenant Jones, the burning question remained: What about those 15,000 guns? What if they fell into Rebel hands with the U.S. capital just 60 miles away?

The answer lay before him in lines of gunpowder twisting throughout the armory and arsenal buildings. Without hope for reinforcements, Jones sent a dispatch to his superiors: he would destroy what he could not defend. Shortly before 10:00 p.m. sentries informed Jones the enemy had reached the outskirts of town. The time to ignite the powder kegs had come.

At the outbreak of the Civil War, arms-making factories such as the U.S. Armory and Arsenal at Harpers Ferry became prime military targets. This antebellum view of the small arsenal building (background), taken from inside the armory gates, is the only known photograph of the structure. In mid-April of 1861 it helped house 15,000 weapons.

1861

Open Fire

$\mathcal{T}$ension was high in Harpers Ferry. The United States had elected a new president, representing a new political party—and the winning candidate did not even appear on the ballot in Harpers Ferry.

When Abraham Lincoln won the Election of 1860, Southerners feared for their future. Lincoln, a Republican, symbolized to white Southerners a nascent Northern political movement that advocated the abolition of slavery. Southerners considered slave ownership a fundamental property right. By February 1861, seven states from the Deep South had seceded from the Union, declaring themselves separate and independent, and forming the Confederate States of America—a union of Southern states, bound together by their unwavering protection of slavery and the preservation of their culture.

Harpers Ferry and Virginia had been in the forefront of the national storm raging over slavery. Abolitionist John Brown had attacked Harpers Ferry 13 months prior to Lincoln's election, choosing the Ferry as the launch pad for his war against slavery. His target was the U.S. Armory and Arsenal and its stockpile of weapons. Deadly battle erupted on Shenandoah and Potomac Streets as Brown's men battled local militia and citizens to control the armory and arsenal. Enraged citizens fought to defend their town; militia and U.S. Marines fought to stave insurrection and regain control of government property; but Brown and his men fought, ultimately, to determine the destiny of a nation and the future of four million enslaved persons.

The U.S. Armory stood as one of the most advanced industrial complexes in America by the 1850s. At its zenith, the armory employed over 400 workers. Wages at the federal armory often doubled the average earning of $300 per year. The Musket Factory—shown here two years prior to John Brown's Raid—comprised 20 industrial buildings that stretched 600 yards along the Potomac River. (Marine Museum, Quantico)

3

Trapped Between the Jaws of North and South

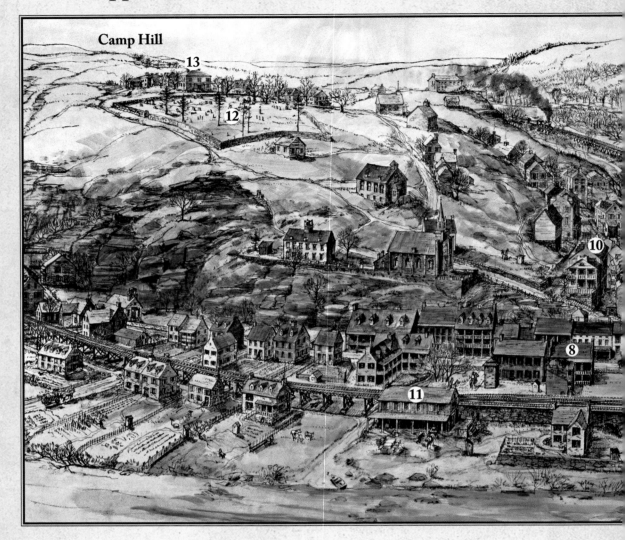

Lower Town Harpers Ferry looking north from Loudoun Heights. Antebellum Harpers Ferry thrived as a bustling industrial town at the confluence of the Potomac and Shenandoah Rivers. Its nearly 3,000 residents comprised a mix of social, political, and cultural differences. Armory workers from Springfield, Massachusetts, mixed their New England upbringing with native Virginians. Travelers on the Baltimore and Ohio Railroad and Chesapeake and Ohio Canal brought transient conversations to the taverns and inns. Irish and German immigrants offered perspectives from different languages, cultures, and religions. Slave owners and nonslaveholders were neighbors. Equal numbers of slaves and free blacks resided in the community. In 1861, these differences tested their loyalties and friendships. Those who reflected the lingering anger and angst of John Brown's Raid embraced secession. Others—especially the armory employees—feared secession would only lead to a war of destruction. They envisioned lost jobs, lost homes, and lost lives.

Located on the border between the United States and Confederate States, many of the town's antebellum structures would be destroyed or utilized for military purposes. (NATIONAL PARK SERVICE, HARPERS FERRY CENTER COMMISSIONED ART COLLECTION, ARTIST RICHARD SCHLECHT, PHOTOGRAPHER ERIC LONG)

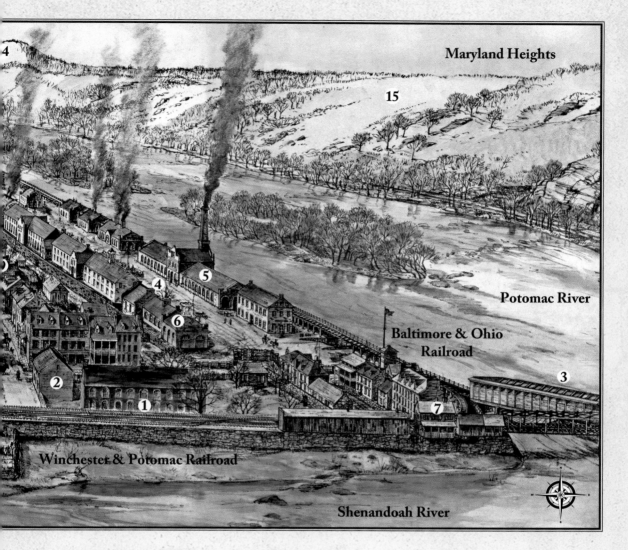

1. Large Arsenal (Burned by U.S. troops at outset of war, April 18, 1861).
2. Small Arsenal (Burned by U.S. troops at outset of war, April 18, 1861).
3. B&O Railroad bridge (Burned and rebuilt nine times in four years).
4. U.S. Amory Musket Factory (Burned by Confederate troops, June 14, 1861).
5. Forge and Smithing Shop (U.S. Quartermaster Depot in March 1862. Burned during three separate Confederate invasions. Main base of supplies for the United States during Sheridan's 1864 Shenandoah Valley Campaign).
6. John Brown's Fort (Occasionally used as a prison, it survived the war).
7. The Point (Structures burned by U.S. troops February 7, 1862, included the Wager House Hotel, the Gault House Saloon, the Winchester and Potomac Depot, and the B&O ticket office).
8. Master Armorer's House (U.S. commanders' headquarters. General U.S. Grant spent the night here on September 17, 1864).
9. Provost Marshal's Office on High Street during U.S. occupation 1863–1865.
10. Annie Marmion's home, where she survived bombardment in July 1864.
11. Market (Goods and supplies marketed here under strict martial law).
12. Harper Cemetery (C.S. artillery position in spring 1861.)
13. Armory Paymaster's House (Used as hospital, prison, headquarters, ballroom, and school for former slaves).
14. Site of U.S. Fort Duncan.
15. Site of U.S. Naval Battery.

John Brown's Battle at Harpers Ferry against Citizen Volunteers and Militia, Oct. 17th, 1859.

"I, John Brown am now quite certain that the crimes of this <u>guilty</u>, <u>land:</u> <u>will</u> never be purged <u>away</u>; but with Blood. I had as <u>I</u> now <u>think</u>: <u>vainly</u> flattered myself that without very much bloodshed; it might be done."

As the Lincoln election and secession created a crisis within the Union, Virginia faced a dilemma. Should it remain in the United States? Or should it cast its future with the Southern slaveholding states?

The Virginia General Assembly voted to establish a special convention to determine its course, with each county represented by two elected delegates. Jefferson County's two delegates supported a pro-Union platform—mirroring the position of all Shenandoah Valley counties and those of western Virginia. Harpers Ferry had a distinct voice in the secession debates, as U.S. Armory Superintendent Alfred M. Barbour served as a pro-Union Jefferson County delegate.

A native of Virginia, Barbour faced a serious predicament. As a civilian employee of the U.S. government, he was responsible for protecting the federal dollars invested in the armory infrastructure and machinery, and the weapons stored in the two arsenal buildings. As early as January 2, 1861, Barbour had received foreboding intelligence. "I have some reason to apprehend that some assault will be made upon the United States Armory," Barbour informed the Chief of Ordnance, his superior in Washington. "My reasons I do not feel at liberty to disclose." His message became dire. "The Armory might be taken and destroyed; the arms might be abstracted and removed or destroyed; vast amount of damage might be done to the Government property." He requested "reliable regularly drilled" soldiers of the U.S. Army be stationed at Harpers Ferry. Washington responded the next day, ordering sixty "Regulars" from the Carlisle Barracks to guard the Harpers Ferry Armory.

Model 1841 Percussion Rifle. Weapons evolved as the Harpers Ferry Armory experimented with new designs that improved the accuracy, dependability, and loading and firing speed of small arms. (NATIONAL PARK SERVICE, DIGITAL IMAGING PROJECT)

As Barbour protected the national interests, Virginia refused to submit to Southern pressure to join the Confederacy. Recognizing its geographic position on the border between North and South would make it a battleground in a civil war, Virginia advocated compromise and patience, invoking the precedence established by the Founding Fathers. Superintendent Barbour reflected this conservative approach, voting time and again against declarations of secession.

Barbour—and Virginia—radically altered their course, however, following the Confederate bombardment and seizure of Fort Sumter in Charleston Harbor, South Carolina. Faced with an act of war, President Lincoln called upon all states remaining in the Union to contribute troops to squash the rebellion. Virginia's quandary: should it support Lincoln or the South? Secession was the response. On April 17, 1861, five days after the shells flew at Sumter, and less than 48 hours after Lincoln's call for troops, Virginia voted 88 to 55 to separate from the United States.

Superintendent Barbour raced to Harpers Ferry to inform the armorers and local citizens of the secession decision. Barbour's bold announcement nearly incited a riot. Some viewed him as a patriot, a son of Virginia, and a hero to the cause of the South. Others declared him a traitor to his government and a person without principles. Barbour pleaded for calm, ensuring that a Virginia in the fledgling Confederacy would guarantee good jobs and secure futures. In the frenzied aftermath of Barbour's announcement, Jeremiah Donovan grabbed a weapon and stood guard at the armory gate. Fifty yards away, John Burk, a strong loyalist to the South, took up arms at the telegraph office. These two angry men warily watched each other, neither willing to flinch. Harpers Ferry—and the nation—were now at war.

Armory Superintendent Alfred M. Barbour (HFNHP)

Opposite page, top: *Local militia units and armed citizens surrounded Brown at the armory's fire engine-house. Eighteen months following Brown's capture many of the same militiamen returned to the Ferry to seize the same weapons that had attracted Brown.* (COURTESY OF HARPERS FERRY NATIONAL HISTORICAL PARK, HARPERS FERRY, WEST VIRGINIA)

Opposite page, bottom: *Abolitionist John Brown attacked Harpers Ferry in October 1859, launching his war against slavery. Brown's raid and his subsequent trial whirled a nation divided by slavery toward civil war.* (HFNHP)

Amidst this mob-like crowd was Lieutenant Roger Jones, commander of the U.S. garrison of 42 troops at Harpers Ferry. Jones's mission was to protect the Federal property. Upon hearing that Virginia intended to seize the Harpers Ferry complex, Jones acted quickly. "I have taken steps which ought to insure my receiving early intelligence of the advance of any forces," Jones informed army headquarters. "My determination is to *destroy* what I cannot defend." With no reinforcements available, and certain his small force could not protect the government works, Jones ordered his soldiers to distribute kegs of gunpowder throughout the armory and arsenal buildings. Then he waited.

On the evening of April 18—less than 24 hours after Virginia seceded—sentries informed Jones that a 3,000-man Virginia militia force had reached Bolivar Heights, just west of Harpers Ferry, and were poised to descend upon the town. At 10:00 p.m., Jones ordered the powder kegs ignited. Explosions rocked residents out of their beds. Windows shattered. The dark sky brightened as flames engulfed the two arsenal buildings. Fires began raging in the armory build-

Roger Jones (LIBRARY OF CONGRESS, PRINTS AND PHOTOGRAPHS ONLINE CATALOG)

ings. Jones reported in "three minutes, or less, both of the arsenal buildings . . . together with the carpenter's shop, which was at the upper end of a long and connected series of workshops of the armory proper, were in a complete blaze."

Desperate to douse the flames and save their jobs and livelihood, workers raced to the armory and fought the flames. Three hundred Virginia militiamen

En route to seize the U.S. Armory and Arsenal, Virginia militiamen secretly gather at Halltown, four miles from Harpers Ferry. (HFNHP)

THE RENDEZVOUS OF THE VIRGINIANS AT HALLTOWN, VIRGINIA, 5 P.M. ON APRIL 18, 1861, TO MARCH ON HARPER'S FERRY.
[SKETCHED BY D. H. STROTHER.]

marched down Washington and High Streets and encountered no opposition as Jones and his men had abandoned the town. They had crossed the Potomac River bridge and were now speeding north through Maryland. The militia arrived too late to salvage the burning arsenals, but they helped quench the fires in the musket factory, saving most of the buildings and machinery. Their commander, the animated Captain Turner Ashby from Fauquier County, lamented the loss of 15,000 weapons in the arsenals, but proclaimed victory in preserving and seizing the more valuable arms-producing machinery.

The next morning an unusual ceremony occurred. Ashby's men hauled down the Stars and Stripes flying over the musket factory and replaced it with the flag of the Commonwealth of Virginia. Harpers Ferry was now a town on the border in a war between the states.

Captain Turner Ashby led the militia that seized Harpers Ferry on the first day of the war in Virginia. (LOC/PPOC)

Top: *Virginia militia doused flames in the armory buildings, saving dozens of machines that later made weapons for the Confederacy.* (FRANK LESLIE'S ILLUSTRATED NEWSPAPER)

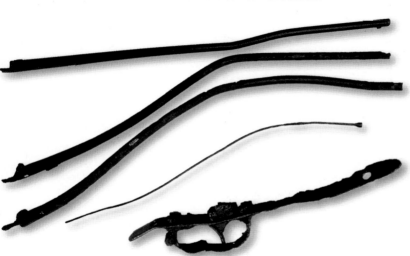

Fragments of barrels and gun parts melted and twisted by the intense heat of the arsenal fires. Archeologists discovered these artifacts nearly 100 years after the burning while excavating the site of the small arsenal. (HFNHP)

9

The destruction of the U.S. Arsenal represented the first property destroyed in Virginia, occurring less than 24 hours after the state seceded. (HARPER'S WEEKLY)

11

The Best Blood of Virginia

*N*ot since the trauma of John Brown's Raid had Harpers Ferry witnessed such pandemonium. Disorder and chaos characterized the first days of military occupation. Individual militia companies, boasting names like the Albemarle Rifles, Monticello Guards, Winchester Continentals, and the Botts Greys streamed into town, most with little preparation. "I was dressed in my best suit ready for church when orders came for me to meet my company at the Armory for duty at once," wrote Sam Buck of Warren County in the heart of the Shenandoah Valley. "I did not even have time to change my clothes." Buck was placed on guard duty over "a lot of old iron that nothing less than a mule team could have moved." Buck explained, "The fact that I was a noncommissioned officer was not taken into consideration, indeed it was all new to us. . . . The lieutenant played sergeant and I private and this was practiced several times before we were posted as to our respective [ranks]." Buck characterized his initiation to the war as a "Sunday soldier," unaware that this was his "start on the slippery and uncertain road to fame."

During the first week of the war militia duties were handled democratically. Military arrangements were discussed, votes taken, resolutions passed, and no authority acknowledged "beyond the will of the majority of the company." Militia generals strutted about in glittering uniforms, seeking the support of their men with offers of whiskey. Sober warriors, when they could be found, stretched battle lines across the town streets as alarm after alarm warned of the approaching enemy. False reports of a Yankee invasion via the B&O Railroad kept the troops in excitement. Soldiers stopped and boarded trains, searching cars for enemy soldiers or their patrons. Between false alarms, company meetings, and occasional drills, the volunteers concentrated on adjusting to army life. "I am very pleasantly quartered in the home of a Catholic Priest," proclaimed E. D. Tracy to his wife. Beds, bunks, and cook stoves soon replaced machinery as some of the armory buildings were converted into comfortable quarters.

The Confederate Stars and Bars flew over Harpers Ferry for the first eight weeks of the war. Southern artillery posted near the Harper Cemetery pointed menacingly at Maryland—a state that still remained within the Union. (FRANK LESLIE'S ILLUSTRATED NEWSPAPER; FLAG: WWW. HISTORICALIMAGEBANK.COM)

"Society was plentiful," observed Henry Kyd Douglas, "for the ranks were filled with the best blood of Virginia." Private Douglas, a practicing attorney now serving in the "Hamtramck Guards" of Shepherdstown, was impressed with the sudden egalitarian aspect of the first days of war. "All the classes were there," serving side-by-side, without notice of usual class distinction. Farmers joined doctors as privates. Teachers marched shoulder-to-shoulder with shoemakers. Laborers drilled daily with student scholars. Both officers and militiamen brought their slaves with them to cook, clean clothes, and keep the camp tidy. Douglas even recalled the glee of "mothers and sisters and other dear girls [coming] constantly to Harper's Ferry and there was little difficulty in seeing them. . . . Nothing was serious yet . . . everything much like a joke."

Thomas Jonathan Jackson
(HFNHP)

At Harpers Ferry, the Potomac River separated the United States from the Confederate States. The B&O Railroad bridge connected the two warring nations. The C&O Canal can be seen in the center of this photo. (NATIONAL GEOGRAPHIC SOCIETY)

The arrival of Thomas Jonathan Jackson abruptly ended this festive atmosphere. Jackson's first command of the Civil War was at Harpers Ferry. Arriving on April 29, he discovered "things presented a most hopeless aspect." The newly commissioned Colonel Jackson, recently teaching physics and artillery drill at the Virginia Military Institute, quickly transformed Harpers Ferry into an army town. Drawing upon his experience as a West Pointer and Mexican War veteran, Jackson disposed of the whiskey and deposed the militia generals. He stripped independence from the individual companies and organized them into regiments. He established the 1st Virginia Brigade, an organization that he commanded and drilled, hardening it so that it soon would stand like a stone wall at the Battle of First Manassas. Within the ranks of Jackson's Brigade, encamped upon the slopes of Bolivar Heights, was Company K, 2nd Virginia Infantry—known locally as the Floyd Guards (named after former Secretary of War John B. Floyd), and commanded by Harpers Ferry Mayor George W. Chambers. Within one week of Jackson's arrival, "the pomp and circumstance of glorious war" had been replaced with seven hours of daily drill, and enforcement of the strictest military code. "What a revolution three or four days had wrought," reported the commander of the Staunton Artillery. "Perfect order reigned everywhere."

Harpers Ferry became a position of strategic importance for the infant Confederacy during the first month of the war. Robert E. Lee, recently named overall commander of Virginia's burgeoning forces and charged with the defense of the Old Dominion, determined that several key areas provided the best protection against expected Federal invasion. Lee selected Harpers Ferry as one important position because it stood at the gateway into the strategic Shenandoah Valley. Lee reasoned his forces must occupy and hold Harpers Ferry, otherwise northwestern Virginia would be lost; Virginia would be sliced in half due to Union occupation of the Valley; and the B&O Railroad would operate unimpeded, funneling troops and supplies east and west for the Northerners. Lee aptly summarized: "As regards Harper's Ferry, its abandonment would be depressing to the cause of the South."

Jackson agreed, but he faced a problem concerning the best position of defense. Maryland Heights, the highest point surrounding the Ferry, loomed over the town from the north bank of the Potomac and its occupation made good strategic sense. The dominating bluffs, however, stood upon Maryland soil; and unlike Virginia, the Old Line State had not yet seceded from the Union. Occupation of Maryland Heights, by some interpretations, represented an invasion of Maryland. Such offensive action could alienate the people of Maryland—and neither Virginia nor the Confederacy could afford to lose this important border state.

Jackson was only briefly deterred by the politics of Maryland Heights. On May 7, he informed Lee: "I have finished reconnoitering the Maryland Heights, and have determined to fortify them at once, and hold them . . . be the cost what it may." Jackson's aggression soon created Virginia's first "diplomatic" incident of the Civil War.

Leaving the "determination" of Maryland Heights in Jackson's hands solicited a rapid response from General Lee. "In your preparation for the defense of your position," Lee warned Jackson on May 9, "it is considered advisable not to intrude upon the soil of Maryland, unless compelled by the necessities of war." Lee's instructions arrived too late, however; for on the same day, Jackson proudly announced that he had occupied Maryland Heights with about 500 soldiers from Virginia and Kentucky. In an effort to mollify politics, Jackson purposely had selected the Kentucky contingent since Kentucky, itself, was a border state. This ploy did not pacify the Marylanders, however, and they reacted with rage.

Even before Jackson's seizure of Maryland Heights, Marylanders residing near the Ferry had complained that Virginia soldiers had forcibly entered private houses, seized personal property, and insulted and threatened "unoffending citizens."

Dr. Augustus A. Biggs, a Maryland Heights property owner aggrieved by Jackson's presence, dashed a letter to Maryland Governor Thomas H. Hicks. Biggs alleged the Southerners had destroyed "a large quantity of timber by fire," and demanded that Maryland seek protection against losses incurred by the "invasion of our State." Biggs' protest, in conjunction with solicitations from other disgruntled Marylanders, prompted the Maryland Committee on Federal Relations to appoint a special "Commissioner to Virginia" to investigate these

"I am of the opinion that this place should be defended with the spirit which actuated the defenders of Thermopylae, and, if left to myself, such is my determination."
—**Colonel Thomas J. Jackson, 1861**

General Robert E. Lee, overall commander in Virginia, selected Harpers Ferry as a strategic point of defense. (LOC/PPOC)

This Confederate stockade was the first fortification on Maryland Heights.
(HARPER'S WEEKLY)

Former U.S. Senator James M. Mason, a resident of the Shenandoah Valley, argued that Virginia had the right to occupy Maryland for self-defense.
(NATIONAL ARCHIVES AND RECORDS ADMINISTRATION)

allegations. Virginia Governor John Letcher—depending upon Maryland's secession to provide security to Virginia's northern border—worked deliberately and diligently to resolve this diplomatic crisis. He promised full and liberal compensation for any property damage caused by troops from the Old Dominion. Letcher also promised that occupation only would occur "in defen[s]e and protection of [Virginia] soil from threatened or actual invasion."

As the legal, ethical, and diplomatic debate raged over the occupation of Maryland Heights, Jackson continued its fortification. Trees were axed and burned atop the crest. In this clearing, a wooden stockade 200 feet long was erected by a Virginia infantry company known as the "Montgomery Fencibles." Slave labor apparently performed some of the mountain work, as accounts in the *Alexandria Gazette* reported 40 to 50 blacks crossing the Potomac River "with axes and picks," and that the "laboring force of Negroes upon Maryland Heights is daily increasing." The *Gazette* concluded: "Colonel Jackson seems to think that the pick and the shovel are great weapons of warfare."

The work on Maryland Heights did, indeed, have military implications. The U.S. government eyed Maryland Heights as a military threat. As U.S. troops mustering in Pennsylvania prepared to pour into Washington County and Hagerstown, Maryland, in the middle of June 1861, the Southern occupation of Maryland Heights and Harpers Ferry posed the nearest threat. Union scouts heard "at night the sound of the hammer . . . breaking stone on the Maryland Heights, the ax felling trees. Evidently a blockhouse is going up. No one can get near enough to see." These reports convinced the Federal sector commander, Major General Robert Patterson, to consider Maryland Heights as a potential battleground. His initial plan recommended a force to "threaten the Maryland Heights," and "should a favorable occasion offer, storm them." Patterson concluded the Rebels' "design on this field [is] to make a desperate struggle for supremacy."

As Jackson's men labored upon Maryland Heights throughout May, he turned his attention to the other heights, determined to bolster his defenses elsewhere. Jackson ordered substantial stone blockhouses constructed on Loudoun Heights—the second highest peak overlooking the Ferry—and on the opposite shore of the Shenandoah. This may have been more psychological than practical, as any enemy approach to Loudoun Heights

THE BATTERY, HARPER'S FERRY.

necessitated an advance through Southern territory. He also erected artillery earthworks on the bluff near the eastern base of the Harper Cemetery—strategically placed to command the town, railroad, Potomac bridge, and the C&O Canal. Nearly two miles west of town, Jackson planted heavy ordnance on a northern plateau on Bolivar Heights, with the menacing cannon facing north. "Our heights are being fortified perfectly," reported a soldier to his home newspaper in Rockingham County, Virginia. "In a few days Harper's Ferry will be a point which all creation cannot take—not only impossible, but impregnable. Let Abraham make the most of that."

Naval cannon seized from the Norfolk Navy Yard arrived via railroad to bolster Bolivar Heights' defenses. A brigade of infantry drills on the plateau. (DRAWING BY D. H. STROTHER FOR *HARPER'S WEEKLY*)

Concerned over the future security of
Harpers Ferry, Virginia, authorities
ordered the captured armory machinery—
similar to this rifling machine—to be
moved further south. (NPS/DIP)

While Jackson secured his position, General Lee also charged him with the removal of the armory machinery to safety. With no guarantee Maryland would secede—and recognizing that the Potomac River could become the international boundary between North and South—the Virginia Secession Convention ordered Governor Letcher on April 25 to remove the machinery. The armorers—concerned they'd have to leave their homes and relocate, or, worse, lose their jobs entirely—voiced their opinions through Thomas M. Isbell, a wealthy (and influential) Jefferson County slaveholder. "The machinery is immense and very valuable, much of which cannot be removed without total loss," Isbell argued. "The armory is now in condition for actual operation, and could in a short time turn out many thousand

Jackson's Great Train Robbery

The operation of the Baltimore and Ohio Railroad irritated Colonel Thomas Jackson, as he suspected the Union leanings of the railroad's chief executive, President John W. Garrett. The wily Jackson, claiming the clamor of the cars and the chugging locomotives interrupted the drill and sleep of his troops, kept restricting the railroad's hours of operation. Garrett had little choice but to abide by Jackson's demands, as the Confederates controlled the railroad bridge spanning the Potomac.

By May 23, railroad operations had been constricted to two hours, from 11:00 a.m. to 1:00 p.m. As Garrett crammed his trains through the time funnel, Jackson sprang his trap, sealing and capturing all rail traffic between Point of Rocks, Maryland, and Martinsburg, Virginia (now West Virginia)—a stretch of nearly 30 miles, with Harpers Ferry near the midpoint. In a literal "great train robbery," Jackson had snatched 56 locomotives and 300 cars

The B&O Railroad proved a tempting target for Colonel Jackson. He seized locomotives and cars similar to the ones pictured here at nearby Martinsburg. (MDHS)

from the unsuspecting B&O Railroad Company. Some of the confiscated property soon became iron horses for the fledging Confederacy.

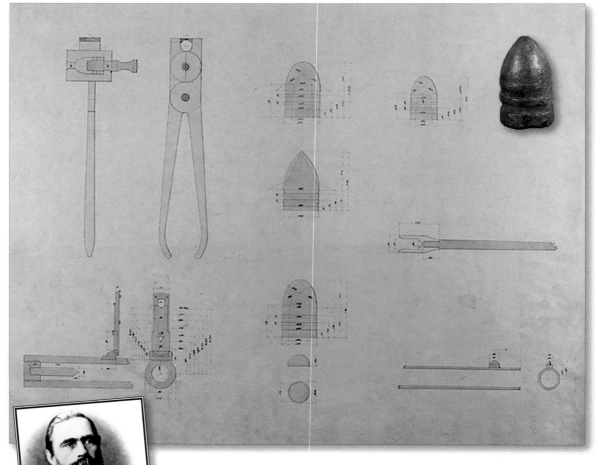

stand of arms. . . . There are a great many unfinished guns here which could be ready for use in a short time if operations are not suspended." Isbell proffered economics: "The cost of taking down, transporting, and re-erecting will be immense." Finally, he pleaded loyalty. "Operatives in all departments are here ready to work, and thus furnish arms for the troops of the State. . . . The workmen here will be as loyal to Virginia as they have ever been to the United States."

Despite Isbell's logic and pleas, Virginia authorities believed the armory could not operate in such a perilous position. General Lee subsequently ordered Colonel Jackson to dismantle the gun-making machinery and ship it south to safer environs. Cargo wagons and freight trains were impressed; and within one week of his arrival at the Ferry, two-thirds of the armory machinery had been moved to Winchester, where it awaited eventual transfer to Richmond and Fayetteville, North Carolina. Thus, Jackson ensured the Harpers Ferry Armory machinery was secured to manufacture rifles and rifle-muskets for the Confederacy. Once the machinery began moving, numerous armory workers offered their skills to the South, following the machinery to their new factories.

The Burton Bullet, also known as the Minié Ball, was perfected at Harpers Ferry by master armorer James H. Burton (inset). Its design enabled the rifle to replace the musket, thus extending the length and accuracy of a projectile from 100 yards to 400 yards. As the principal bullet of the Civil War, it increased casualties dramatically. Burton took his skills to the Confederacy, eventually becoming superintendent of the Macon, Georgia arsenal. (NPS/DIP; HFNHP)

The Eerie Silence of Destruction

By the third week of May, the force at Harpers Ferry had burgeoned beyond 8,000 men, including troops from as far away as Mississippi, Alabama, Tennessee, and Kentucky. "It is the prettiest sight in the world to see them drilling," wrote Charles R. Norris, a cadet at the Virginia Military Institute who had been assigned to Harpers Ferry to assist with instruction. "The troops here are getting in a pretty good state of discipline and we will give Old Abe's troops a pretty hard shake." E. D. Tracy from Huntsville, Alabama, was also confident. "I do not believe there will be any attack, but if there be, we'll whip the rascals back to their dens." Rumors of attack became a daily, irritating occurrence. "We have got used to such things," commented a Rockingham County correspondent. "The idea seems to prevail that we are often called out just to see who will be first out. Of course that stimulates rivalry."

Rivalry also existed between Confederate leaders. Men that began their careers at Harpers Ferry would have many disagreements over the course of the war. Thomas J. Jackson himself caused or fomented some of these feuds. Future Southern generals who led their first commands at Harpers Ferry included J. E. B. Stuart, Turner Ashby, A. P. Hill, William Nelson Pendleton, and John Imboden. In fact, Confederate President Jefferson Davis believed a general should command at Harpers Ferry, so he assigned Brigadier General Joseph E. Johnston the post, where he arrived on May 23, 1861. Colonel Jackson subordinated himself to Johnston, and Jackson turned strictly to the direction of his 1st Virginia Brigade.

Almost immediately, General Johnston quibbled with Lee in his assessment of Harpers Ferry's importance. "Considered as a position," Johnston informed Lee, "I regard Harper's Ferry as untenable."

Lee protested, and ultimately sought help from a higher authority. "The importance of the subject has induced me to lay it before the President [Davis]," Lee notified Johnston. "He places great value upon our retention of the command of the Shenandoah Valley and the position at Harper's Ferry." Johnston refused to yield. Admitting insubordination, the general later declared: "Not withstanding this determination on the part of the Executive, I resolved not to continue to occupy the place."

Thus on June 13, three weeks after his arrival, Johnston ordered the evacuation of Harpers Ferry. As his command marched toward Winchester, Johnston instructed that the armory buildings and the railroad bridge be destroyed. Flames scorched the musket factory structures on June 14 and 15, and the majestic covered bridge—the pride of the B&O Railroad—exploded into burning timbers and ash at 6:30 a.m. on June 14. "The whole bridge was sprinkled with camphor," recorded David Hunter Strother in his private journal. "The span next to the Wager House was blown up to prevent setting fire to the town in that quarter." Strother then provided this

Joseph E. Johnston ordered the Confederate evacuation of Harpers Ferry. (NARA)

Artist and writer David Hunter Strother, a resident of nearby Martinsburg, witnessed the destruction of the arsenal at war's onset and the burning of the railroad bridge. He returned to the town throughout the war as a Union officer, recording its worsening condition. (LOC/PPOC)

eyewitness account of the bridge destruction: "The whole structure seemed to ignite at once and was soon consumed, the incombustible parts, iron rails and metal roofing, falling into the water, the quantity of half-burned timber and there forming a dam the whole way over that one might cross upon. . . . As it burned the blazing camphor poured down into the river and floated off burning upon the surface." Strother noted that the trestlework near the Wager House was spared so as not to endanger the hotel property.

General Johnston also ordered the torching of the wagon bridges at Point of Rocks and Berlin (now Brunswick), Maryland, and Shepherdstown, Virginia. Although designed to prevent easy crossing of the river by the Federals, this effectively severed civilian trade and intercourse between Maryland and Virginia on this section of the Potomac. Two weeks later, the Confederates returned to Harpers Ferry to finish their destruction, blowing up the covered bridge spanning the Shenandoah and igniting and gutting the rifle factory on Hall's Island.

Remnants of the hasty Confederate evacuation littered the Harpers Ferry environs. As Strother rummaged about, he noticed on Bolivar Heights seven "heavy cannon spiked [and] the truck platforms and sand bags burnt, cannon balls lying around the quantity of powder which had been emptied into the bushes." Across Bolivar Heights he discovered "deserted camp brush sheds and tents strew with old papers, old boots, canteens, camp kettle, and a quantity of refuse and decayed [food] over which the buzzards were floating."

Confederates evacuated their artillery position on Camp Hill in mid-June 1861. During the next three years, Harpers Ferry would change hands seven more times. (HARPER'S WEEKLY)

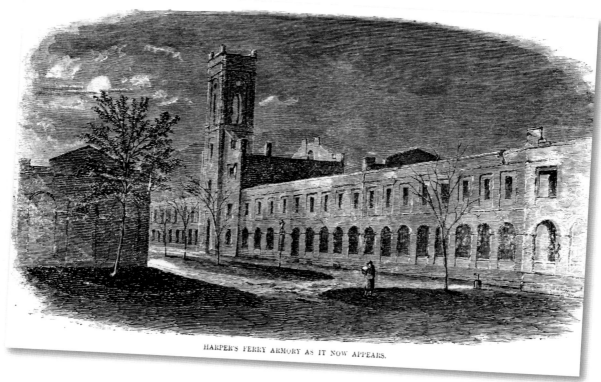

HARPER'S FERRY ARMORY AS IT NOW APPEARS.

A particular curiosity for Strother was the former armory superintendent's quarters. Recently vacated by General Johnston as his headquarters, "it seemed to have suffered more than any other and stood open, the locks broken, furniture removed and the floors and grounds strewed with papers, topographical plans, letters, and paymaster's rolls. . . . People were walking about through the building apparently seeking what they might pick up." Strother spied something in the Potomac, too. "I saw where two thousand bushels of corn was emptied into the river. The corn was visible for some distance under the water like golden sand."

Surprised by the sudden and unexpected Confederate withdrawal from Harpers Ferry, Union Major General Robert Patterson recommended that his army—now concentrated around Hagerstown—establish a stronghold in enemy territory and utilize the Ferry as a headquarters, depot, and base of operations. Patterson further proposed as a "military necessity" the reconstruction of the B&O Railroad bridge at Harpers Ferry. According to the general, this would reopen the east-west line of communication, protect the channel of trade, and remedy transportation and supply problems

Ruins of burned Musket Factory. (Harper's Weekly)

The Rifle Factory along the Shenandoah following the thorough work of Confederate torchbearers. (HFNHP)

General Robert Patterson commanded the first United States occupation of Harpers Ferry. (LOC/PPOC)

for his army. Patterson concluded, "Until Harper's Ferry is occupied and fortified I should fear the return of the rebels."

But on June 19, Patterson reported the railroad company balked at his plan, refusing to rebuild the bridge until the entire line west to Cumberland received adequate Federal protection. Stung by the B&O's counter and lack of cooperation, Patterson decided that he would not occupy Maryland Heights, but direct attention instead on his nemesis General Johnston, now at Winchester.

The Confederate abandonment and change in Union plans heralded a period of uncertainty in Harpers Ferry. Now free of military occupiers, town resident Frederick Roeder observed: "Well, we have got rid of that lot and have escaped with our lives, but what will the next party that comes do with us?" With the armory in ruins and the government jobs gone, economic hardship strangled the town. Businesses closed, the streets became empty, and people moved away. Commerce virtually ceased, as the railroad no longer operated and the canal struggled to survive. Without the grinding machinery, whirling turbines, slapping belts, whistles and bells—and

The Indiscriminate Bullet

Civil War bullets did not discriminate between friend and foe, or for that matter, between soldier and civilian. Harpers Ferry resident Frederick Roeder fell victim to this new terror of everyday life.

The first skirmish between Blue and Gray soldiers in Harpers Ferry happened on July 4, 1861. After about 30 minutes the shooting stopped; the Rebels departed. Curious about the fighting, respected businessman and confectioner Roeder walked toward the railroad office near the Point—at the time a crowded commercial area where the two rivers converged. Believing the danger had passed, Roeder made no attempt to disguise his presence. Tense Federals on the Maryland side continued their vigilant watch, with fingers on triggers. As Roeder neared the Fouke Hotel, a Federal bullet intended for another onlooker ricocheted off the building and ripped a hole in his groin. Roeder struggled back to his home on High Street, where he died surrounded by his family.

The first civilian killed in Harpers Ferry, ironically, was a staunch Union man, cut down with a Union bullet, on the Union's favorite day of celebration.

German immigrant Frederick Roeder ran a bakery and sweets shop out of his home (left) on High Street. Accidentally shot during the town's first skirmish, he died at his home surrounded by family. (NPS, PHOTOGRAPHER MARSHA WASSEL)

few people talking—an eerie silence pervaded. "A dead calm reigned," recalled resident Joseph Barry. "The stillness was rendered oppressive."

Although the Federal army did not occupy the town, officials in Washington became concerned that a void of U.S. troops in the Harpers Ferry sector could invite Confederate incursions into Maryland. Subsequently, during the first week of July, the first Union infantry companies appeared on the north bank of the Potomac, based at nearby Sandy Hook. Troops from the 1st Pennsylvania and the 9th New York took positions along the C&O Canal and atop the cliffs on Maryland Heights. When sector commander Colonel Charles P. Stone arrived on July 3 to inspect his new line, he spied across the river into the town. "Harper's Ferry appears to be deserted," he reported. "I could see but half a dozen people in the town without my glass."

That changed abruptly the next day. "Harper's Ferry was suddenly occupied by a few of the enemy, who opened fire on our pickets." With those words, Charles Stone recorded the first engagement of the Civil War at Harpers Ferry. It was Independence Day, 1861. The war was 10 weeks old. For about 30 minutes, bullets hissed across the Potomac. Stone reported one Union soldier killed in action and three wounded. Two Confederates were killed and two severely wounded.

A Melancholy Ruin

The sturdy wood-covered B&O Railroad bridge carried tons of freight and passenger trains across the Potomac for 22 years, but it would meet its demise after only two months of civil war. (*Harper's Weekly*) Top Inset: The covered bridge looking down the Potomac. (MDHS) Bottom Inset: B&O Engine Number 169 became a casualty of the Confederate evacuation, thrown from the railroad bridge during its destruction. (*Harper's Weekly*)

"Before us lay the great railroad bridge; a melancholy ruin, the blackened beams, the piers reddened with intense heat, the whole of the magnificently built workshops of Government buildings a mass of scarred and smoking ashes. . . . The work of destruction was as complete as human malignity could make it."

—Baltimore American and Commercial Advertiser

Remains of the B&O Railroad bridge soon after its destruction. (HFNHP)

The Seven-Day Occupation

When the 2nd Massachusetts Infantry marched into Harpers Ferry on July 18, the "Harvard Regiment" was greeted with a pleasant surprise. "Men, women, and children cheering us, waving flags, and evidently overjoyed to see United States troops again," wrote Charles Morse. Alonzo H. Quint, chaplain of the unit, recorded: "We were welcomed with joy. To see tears rolling down many a cheek at the sight of the old flag was a pleasant sight after the sullen hate of the other [Virginia] places we had been."

Colonel George Gordon, commander of the 2nd Massachusetts, remembered his Harpers Ferry reception. "The citizens gathered in our pathway and shouted, 'Welcome!' Wreaths of flowers were thrown to the troops, and garlands encircled the neck of the horse that bore the commanding officer. We entered as conquerors receiving an ovation. Our band played its most patriotic airs, while the streets rang with shouts of the multitude."

The patriotic women of Harpers Ferry had secretly made a United States flag during the Rebel occupation, hiding it with hopes that someday they could present it to the first Union regiment that entered the town. On July 24, they presented the Stars and Stripes to the 2nd Massachusetts. "Thankful that you have come here to protect our homes and our firesides," rejoiced spokeswoman Annie Marlatt, "and in view of your kind and manly bearing toward us, we . . . take pleasure in presenting you this banner." When the band played *The Star-Spangled Banner* it "filled and swelled in every heart as the color-bearer accepted the offering."

Although pleased with the presentation of colors, Chaplain Quint was more fascinated by Harpers Ferry's encounter with John Brown. "Many curiously examined every place famous for John Brown's footsteps. . . . Chief in interest was the engine-house," where John Brown had made his stand. "I recognized it from the pictures then published . . . there still remains, unaltered, the several holes made through the brick walls, to enable the besieged to fire on their assailants." Inspired by Brown's "Fort," Quint wrote: "The free North is pouring down its sons by hundreds of thousands—in no war to abolish slavery, it is true, but none the less to insure its doom. . . . Had the South remained loyal, slavery would still have been protected. It is now *too late*." In his final thoughts, Quint prophesized: "If our government be wise, besides its immense armies, in the fear of the Southern heart John Brown's ghost is worth a hundred thousand men."

Returning from his reflections, Quint peered at the empty armory buildings. "The long lines of noble shops were mainly in ghastly ruins; the very trees of that once beautiful spot, scorched to death, cast the shadows of their leafless limbs upon the blackened walls." But then Quint noticed something peculiar. "By some chance, the only building of that vast series which still remains uninjured, is the engine-house . . . and over it still wave the green trees, unhurt. Is it a prophetic emblem?"

Removal of a tattered
Confederate flag atop the
90-foot flagpole at the
armory. (HARPER'S WEEKLY)

The first full-scale Federal occupation of Harpers Ferry occurred on July 21 with the arrival of General Robert Patterson's army of 6,000 men. Patterson planted his headquarters flag at the former armory superintendent's residence, whose yard was the bivouac of the 2nd Massachusetts. That same day—nearly 50 miles distant—the first major battle of the Civil War unfolded at Manassas. The 70-year-old Patterson had been duped by the Rebels, failing in his mission to keep the Confederates at Winchester from uniting with the Southern force at Manassas. As the battle raged along the banks of Bull Run, Patterson's troops stood idly along the banks of the Potomac, missing the Civil War's first significant engagement.

"Now the churches are mainly shut up. The schools are abandoned. The sidewalks and streets are rough and ragged. . . . Many houses are deserted. Property, often their little all, is valueless. Their incomes are destroyed with the government shops. . . . Harper's Ferry is ruined."

—Alonzo H. Quint, Chaplain, 2nd Massachusetts

The chagrined Patterson was honorably discharged. Prior to his departure he received a visit from some property owners. Thirteen fugitive slaves had accompanied Patterson's force to Harpers Ferry, seeking Federal protection. Their owners came for them, demanding their return. Since the military was under strict orders at this time not to interfere with slavery, General Patterson ordered "that the masters have all assistance." The fugitives were sent back to their owners. Not all slaves were turned away, however. Several weeks later, Edwin Bryant, from his encampment upon Maryland Heights in the 3rd Wisconsin Infantry, noticed "colored men flocked to our camp and were anxious to be cooks, servants, anything." When an order arrived prohibiting the harboring of slaves in camp, Bryant remembered: "The slaves were turned out of camp in obedience to the order, but were supplied with provisions and started northward to the Pennsylvania border."

The 2nd Massachusetts had its own form of rebellion—not over the merits of abolition—but payment for its services. The Bay State Boys had mustered in the army in early May, but had not received a cent. This intolerable situation inspired a mutiny in early August. "Arms were stacked in the company streets, and when the orderlies ordered the companies to fall in for roll call, most of the men flatly refused," admitted Private John Anderson. When informed of the mutineers the regiment's commander, Colonel George H. Gordon, promptly buckled on his sword, grabbed his loaded revolver, and ordered his staff to follow, hurrying to the stage of insubordination. "With military bearing . . . he folded his arms and demanded in tones of thunder" to hear about any complaints.

After assuring the aggrieved that he understood their wants and assuaging them that he would take care of them, Colonel Gordon inquired, "Do you understand the penalty of your rebellion?" Not waiting for an answer, Gordon delivered his own. "I will tell you that it is death! And now I tell you as sure as there is a God in Heaven if this thing occurs again I will have you surrounded with troops and by order of a court martial shot." Anderson concluded: "I think the men were impressed, for the thing never did occur again."

Not all was serious for the rank and file. From "Camp Wooster" on Maryland Heights, the colonel of the 5th Connecticut Infantry issued permission for his boys to enjoy themselves on Sunday mornings following the 6:00 a.m. inspection of quarters, arms, and equipments. "The men will be allowed two hours for bathing instead of one—and they will be permitted to go to the river if they prefer." To further this emphasis on hygiene and health, the colonel warned the water was for bathing, not drinking: "[Men] are forbidden to carry their canteens with them."

"Hucksters" were forbidden in the camp on the Sabbath, but they could sell their wares any other day as long as they were at least 40 paces outside the front of the camp. "Washerwomen hucksters will not be permitted to pass the lines without exhibiting a written permit from the commanding officer of the regiment." The colonel also ruled against one favorite pastime. "All playing of cards for money in this Regiment is henceforth forbidden."

In the aftermath of the Union disaster at the Battle of First Bull Run, Washington authorities replaced the old professional soldier Patterson with a professional politician. Major General Nathaniel P. Banks, an ardent Republican from Massachusetts and former Speaker of the House in the U.S. Congress, assessed his new assignment: "Twenty thousand men is the least force that can hold this place against a probable attack." The new general preferred an alternative. Instead of holding the town where a bridgeless river disrupted his line of communications into Maryland, Banks believed he should transfer his army to the north bank of the Potomac. With his headquarters at nearby Sandy Hook, he could be supplied by the railroad and have his depot in a secure area. He also could deploy a force on Maryland Heights that "will make the town absolutely untenable by the enemy." Thus, General Banks moved across the river, and the first Union occupation of Harpers Ferry ended only seven days after it had started. "A silence deep as that of an Arabian desert brood[ed] over the place," wrote Joseph Barry, "broken only by the stealthy step of some petty thief engaged in picking up stray articles belonging to the army or to the citizens who had fled in every direction."

General Nathaniel Banks (LOC)

Border Town

*L*ife in Harpers Ferry swung like a pendulum following the Northern vacancy. General Banks' stay at Sandy Hook was short. In mid-August he moved his headquarters to Frederick, Maryland. Banks left behind one corps to prevent the Southerners from crossing the river, to protect the canal and fords in the vicinity, and to eliminate travel, communication, and trade between Maryland and Virginia. During September and October two companies of the 13th Massachusetts Infantry were posted directly opposite Harpers Ferry, along the canal and atop Maryland Heights. After establishing headquarters in a canal boat named *Charles McCardell*, moored near C&O Lock 33, these ever-vigilant Bay-Staters watched Harpers Ferry with eagle eyes. Without warning, one of their rifle shots often broke the silence and echoed from mountain to mountain. Confederate raiding parties or

John Brown's Bell

Scavenging for souvenirs became a sport as fancied as shooting at "secesh." Souvenir hunting reached its zenith in Harpers Ferry when the men of the 13th Massachusetts Regiment decided to appropriate the bell from the cupola of the John Brown Fort. The former armory's fire alarm hung in the cupola of the engine house. Since others "had appropriated everything of value," the Massachusetts contingent decided upon a practical prize—they would seize the bell and send it home to the fire department, as the hook and ladder company had no ringer. The operation commenced on September 26, 1861, when Lieutenant David L. Brown and 15 others from Company I procured a rope, climbed to the roof of the engine house, disconnected the bell from the belfry, and proceeded to lower it. Then, near disaster. Just as the bell reached the edge of the roof, "the rope parted and the bell dropped, striking on a flagstone." Mortified, the collectors rushed to examine their fallen artifact. It did not crack like the Liberty Bell, but a few pieces chipped from the flange— and not enough to tenor the tone of the bell.

With their treasure now secured, the men placed the John Brown Bell first upon a riverboat, and then upon a canal barge for transport to the regiment's headquarters in Williamsport, Maryland. Here the bell remained for 31 years. Finally, in 1892, veterans of the 13th Massachusetts came searching for their bounty, discovering it miraculously on the farm where they had left it three decades before. The bell then traveled to Marlborough, Massachusetts, where it promptly adorned the local post of the Grand Army of the Republic. The John Brown Bell hangs in Marlborough yet today—a symbol to descendants of the "War of the Rebellion"—and is considered by them in value "second only to the famed Liberty Bell."

The bell from the belfry of the John Brown Fort remains today a prized artifact of war, still on display in the hometown of the Massachusetts men who apprehended it. (Courtesy Rick Farrell)

malicious marauders would sometimes ride into town, attract the attention of the Massachusetts sentries, and for sport, exchange long-distance fire. Skirmishes like this made the soldiers and civilians in Harpers Ferry suspect. "Everything that moved about the streets they shot at vindictively," recalled Joseph Barry. "The appearance of even a mullein leaf swaying in the wind elicited a volley . . . and it was lucky for the place that they were indifferent marksmen, else it would have been wholly depopulated."

The Massachusetts boys also deployed a more nefarious weapon than their rifle-muskets. After discovering "two old twelve pound ship cannon" in the area, several enterprising soldiers mounted the pieces and then "wired railroad spikes together" as the projectiles. "We fired several times at Loudoun Heights," recalled Corporal Austin C. Stearns. "A few spikes reached the shore, but the greater part fell into the river. . . . They served for a scare if nothing more."

Nights proved to be harrowing for the Harpers Ferry residents. As summer days shortened and autumn darkness grew longer, even a simple light at night could be hazardous. "Lights of every kind [were] regarded as signals to the Rebels [and] were usually greeted by a volley of guns," recalled grade-schooler Annie Marmion, whose family lived in a row of buildings distinctly visible from Maryland Heights. "The great objects in life were to procure something to eat and to keep yourself out of sight by day, and your lamps or rather candle light hidden by night." Annie witnessed firsthand how any source of light had the potential to end a life. One evening, a lady guest on her way to her bedroom carefully concealed a candle "behind her ample skirts and person." She passed a window just as a gust of wind blew her skirts and the curtain aside. "Shots immediately announced that the light had been seen." Fortunately, the missiles missed.

Southern sympathizers who remained in the town scorned the Northern intruders. They considered them invaders of

their soil, usurpers of their rights, plunderers of their property, traitors to the Founding Fathers, and criminals against the Constitution. The bluecoats showed little tolerance for the more verbose citizens. "There was a most violent secessionist who kept a drug store in the Ferry," recalled Corporal Stearns, "who at all times never failed to show his hatred toward us." As the offensive language hardened, "his insults were unbearable, so one day . . . proceeding to his store, we commenced to clean it out. We made a clean sweep of everything he had and carried it across the river. . . . We saw no more of the druggist."

A Federal soldier's name and regiment etched into stone on Maryland Heights. (Courtesy John C. Frye)

Perhaps no town in America suffered the trials and tribulations of war more than Harpers Ferry during the late summer and fall of 1861. Other towns in Virginia had been occupied, but occupiers provided stability, security, and law. Martial law guaranteed no rights, but it did assure military order. Disorder reigned in Harpers Ferry, affecting all citizens regardless of allegiance. "Few were more uncomfortably situated during the Civil War than the people who lived on the border where the power of one Army ended and the authority of the other began," surmised Annie Marmion. "Where sometimes one had control; sometimes the other; and often times neither." Most could not sustain this suspense and uncertainty. The population of Harpers Ferry was "speedily reduced to less than twenty families."

The early euphoria for war had evaporated by the fall of 1861. The war, now at 180 days and counting, already had lasted much longer than the 90 days predicted by the politicians. The Massachusetts soldiers crowning Maryland Heights and covering the canal could not return home, nor could the citizens, shopkeepers, and farmers of Harpers Ferry. The blackened town presented "a ghost of its former life," noted one observer. Another soldier declared: "the entire place is not actually worth $10."

Opposite page, top: *Grade-schooler Annie Marmion remained with her family in Harpers Ferry throughout the war, experiencing daily dangers and the rigors of survival.* (From book *Under Fire* by Annie Marmion)

Opposite page, bottom: *Buildings like Marmion Row, elevated above the rest of the town, were easy targets for Federal soldiers crouched along the C&O Canal.* (NPS, Photographer Marsha Wassel)

A Union Man at Heart

One place did exist that exceeded the $10 limit—Abraham Herr's flour mill. Prior to the outbreak of war, Herr's Mill was the most prosperous private industry in Harpers Ferry. Located on Virginius Island, and poised at the gateway to the Shenandoah Valley—Virginia's most fertile grain-producing region—Herr's operation received shipments of wheat on the Winchester and Potomac Railroad. The grain was ground into flour and forwarded in barrels to Baltimore via the B&O Railroad. Since Baltimore was the second largest port city in the South prior to the Civil War, Herr commanded top dollar for his farmer suppliers and his bustling business. The Confederate destruction of the B&O bridge in June severed Herr's connection with Baltimore, but his suppliers—the Valley farmers—continued sending their summer yields to his mill. Most predicted

Abraham Herr's massive mill (center) ground golden wheat into white flour, and it flourished as one of the Shenandoah Valley's largest flour mills during the antebellum period. (HFNHP)

the war would be short, so the railroad disruption would be temporary. Meanwhile, Herr had accumulated thousands of bushels of wheat and hundreds of barrels of flour with no where to send it.

For Southern military planners who thought long-term and strategically, the grain at Herr's Mill equaled meals for thousands of Confederate soldiers—the probable reason that Herr's Mill had escaped the Rebel torch. But with the wheat and flour so near the border, the Federal presence could threaten Southern access to these provisions. If Confederate cavalry patrols could keep the Yankees away, the Rebels eventually could move the flour barrels south to a more secure location. Hence, Lieutenant Colonel Turner Ashby's Southern cavalry instituted "a border guard to protect the growing crops, and what remained of the old ones, from Federal use or destruction." Confederate patrols "raised for the special defense of Jefferson County," and under Jefferson natives Captain John Henderson and Captain Robert Baylor, made regular forays into the Ferry to keep the enemy away from the cache.

The Federals intended to either seize the wheat and flour for themselves or destroy it. Men from the 2nd Massachusetts Infantry were sent to retrieve the flour on August 17, following General Banks' departure from the Ferry. This force successfully removed 700 barrels of finished flour to the Maryland side and destroyed a large part of 25,000 bushels of wheat and 15,000 bushels of horse feed. Two days later, irate Confederates arrived "just in time to see their seven hundreds barrels of superfine flour about starting along the Chesapeake and Ohio Canal for Washington [c]ity." Colonel Gordon proclaimed of his unit's first engagement: "We had a lively time for half an hour." He suffered no casualties during the long-range firing across the Potomac. "It was all about the flour, of course."

Colonel John W. Geary, who commanded U.S. troops in the Harpers Ferry sector during the war's first fall and winter, determined to remove or destroy bushels of wheat and barrels of flour at Herr's Mill on Virginius Island. (LOC)

On August 20, the Federals, intending to ensure Herr's Mill would produce no more flour, returned to the Ferry side to permanently disable the shafts, belts, and machinery. The Yankees accomplished their mission by thrusting an iron bar into the spinning cogs. This resulted in a fatal mechanical crash, "followed by a tremor as when a giant dies from a mortal thrust." Pleased with this effort, Colonel Gordon proudly predicted that "Herr's famous flour-mills were useless for the war."

Ironically, Abraham Herr was a Union loyalist. The first destruction of private industry at Harpers Ferry—by the hands of United States soldiers—affected an entrepreneur who was a "Union man at heart." Yet Herr's loss was not total. His mill building had not been destroyed, his machinery had not been removed, and his bushels of wheat remained largely intact. Herr's Mill was inoperable, but not out of business.

Federal incursions across the Potomac greatly irritated the Virginians on the border. "They fire at every man, woman, child, or horse that passes the river upon [our] side," reported sector commander Ashby at the end of September. Colonel Ashby also regretted that he had "no defined instructions as to policy to be pursued towards the enemy in this locality." This lack of Confederate policy and presence created havoc along the Upper Potomac. "The enemy are constantly not only committing depredations, but doing everything in their power to debauch the minds of our people off from their allegiance and loyalty to the South," wrote Andrew Hunter on October 5. The respected resident of Charles Town and the prosecutor of John Brown complained harshly to the Confederate Secretary of War: "[They] are making their boldest inroads upon us, plundering, insulting females, and keeping the whole border for miles into the interior in a state of uneasiness and alarm."

Apprehension and frustration finally produced a letter to President Jefferson Davis. "The enemy crossed the Potomac at Harper's Ferry last week, and in considerable numbers," informed Jefferson County community leader James L. Ranson on October 15. "The enemy have long been in possession of Harper's Ferry, desecrating our soil, pillaging our defenseless and loyal people, and outraging the sanctity of helpless and loyal families." Ranson assured President Davis the "men of this vicinity at last are showing signs of resistance, and I do hope we shall be able to give a good account of the rascals."

This Southern outrage was incited by the Union's removal of wheat from Herr's Mill. The first Federal foray had retrieved flour, but nearly 20,000 bushels of golden grain still remained at the Virginius Island grist mill. When the Unionists returned to Herr's Mill in force on October 8 and commenced ferrying the wheat across the Potomac, local Confederates witnessed their summer harvest disappearing and their winter food falling into enemy possession.

For one week, United States troops from the 3rd Wisconsin Infantry and the 13th Massachusetts had been evacuating the grain. Expecting a possible Rebel reaction, reinforcements arrived from the 28th Pennsylvania Infantry. Two cannon from the 1st Rhode Island Artillery were planted upon Maryland Heights. Union commander Colonel John W. Geary now had 600 soldiers involved in or protecting the grain-removal operation. Nor was that enough. "All the citizens and negroes that could be found were employed," recalled Corporal Austin Stearns of the 13th Massachusetts, who described the burdensome process. "Company I was at the mill to sack the wheat, teams drew it to the river, it was then ferried across and loaded into canal boats."

By the evening of October 15, Geary was satisfied the mission had been accomplished. Since darkness had fallen, he permitted the men to remain one more night in the Ferry, with a scheduled pull out in the morning. During the "delightful moonlight night," the officer of the day reported before dawn that "all had been quiet during the night."

Virginius Island families such as this one (shown here in 1865) were at the mercy of the occupying army throughout the four years of the war. (HFNHP)

The Battle of Bolivar Heights

*E*verything was far from quiet in nearby Charles Town. A woman had arrived at the camp of Turner Ashby with some important intelligence. The previous night she had "swam the Shenandoah to let us know that the enemy were being re-enforced, and the first aim would be to destroy our woolen factories along the Shenandoah and our large flouring mills." Ashby's own force had doubled in the past week, under orders from Confederate authorities in response to the pleas from the border. Nearly 300 infantry militia had arrived from Shenandoah County, though armed with antiquated flintlock muskets. The cavalry had been bolstered to 230, and two artillery pieces had joined the command. Emboldened by his newfound strength, Ashby determined to strike.

The first major engagement of the Civil War at Harpers Ferry commenced at 7:30 a.m. on Wednesday, October 16, 1861. Bullets grazed Federal pickets on Bolivar Heights in the dim light of dawn. Barely visible were three columns of Confederates advancing rapidly from the direction of Charles Town. Geary deployed to block the three principal routes toward the Ferry—leaning his left on the Shenandoah, his center atop Bolivar Heights, and his right protecting the Potomac. Ashby's men pressed forward, driving the bluecoats backward, until reaching the outskirts of the village of Bolivar. The Rebel cavalry, supported by Ashby's infantry militia and two cannon, charged three times—"increasing in impetuosity with each repetition"—but were checked each time by the defenders from Wisconsin, Massachusetts, and Pennsylvania.

A fanciful rendering of the Union capture of abandoned Confederate cannon during the Battle of Bolivar Heights.
(HFNHP, Sketch by Thomas Nast)

A three-hour stalemate ended at approximately 11:00 a.m. when Federals arrived with reinforcements, seizing the Rebel flank along the Potomac edge of the line. Seeing this as "the key to the success of the action," Colonel Geary ordered an attack along his entire front. This forced a gradual Confederate withdrawal, during which the Southerners left behind one cannon with a broken axle. By 1:30 p.m., the Federals were "in possession of the heights from river to river." Soon the colors of the 28th Pennsylvania Volunteers was unfurled "on the soil of Virginia, and planted on an eminence of Bolivar Heights."

Geary claimed his "victory was complete." Ashby, too, was pleased, as the U.S. forces withdrew from Harpers Ferry that night, clearing that region of invaders. Despite all the bullets and cannonading, neither side suffered many casualties. During the night following the fight, Colonel Geary visited the iron foundry at Shenandoah City (just upstream from Virginius Island), where he ascertained it was "used by the rebels for casting shot and shell of all kinds." He promptly ordered the foundry burned that night. Two days later, Confederate cavalry crept onto Virginius Island and torched Herr's Mill. Two of the Ferry's mighty water-powered industries now stood in ruins—testaments to civil war on the border.

(Map by Gene Thorp © 2000)

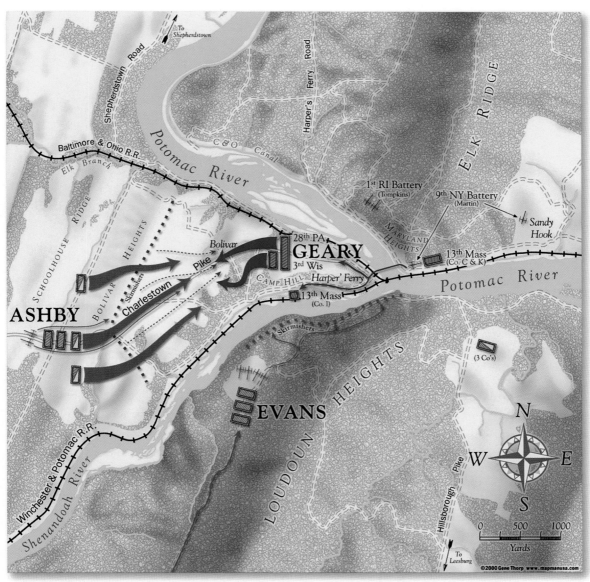

The outcome of the Bolivar Heights battle went far beyond the local battlefield. On October 21, the Confederate Secretary of War responded to "the constant appeals of the inhabitants that we should send a perfectly reliable officer for their protection." He promptly informed Brigadier General Thomas J. "Stonewall" Jackson that he would be assigned to the Shenandoah Valley to protect "the exposed condition of the Virginia frontier." Jackson—the hero of First Manassas—was elated to return home to his beloved Valley. "I have to express my grateful acknowledgement of the honor conferred, and my readiness promptly to comply with the order." Jackson's reentry into the Valley would ultimately change the course of the war the following spring.

John W. Geary, center, claimed victory at the Battle of Bolivar. He is pictured here with his staff, taken during a return to Harpers Ferry the next year. (LOC/PPOC)

Stonewall Jackson's arrival could not come soon enough. "The condition of our border is becoming more alarming every day," reported Alexander R. Boteler, a former United States Congressman who represented the Jefferson County region prior to the outbreak of war. "No night passes without some infamous outrage upon our loyal citizens." In addition to incursions by invaders, Boteler also worried about the growing effect of disloyalty to the Confederacy in the counties bordering the Potomac. "These counties are infested with traitors. . . . They cannot be controlled or guarded against unless someone be invested with authority to deal with them as they deserve. They defy all authority now, and are in daily communication with the enemy."

This rising temperature of Southern emotion manifested itself on the Bolivar Heights battlefield. During the fight, according to the official

report filed by Colonel Geary, four Northern soldiers who were already killed were "afterwards charged upon by the cavalry and stabbed through the body, stripped of all their clothing, not excepting their shoes and stockings, and left to perfect nudity." Geary's troops discovered one of the dead soldiers "laid in the form of a crucifixion, with his hands spread out, and cut through the palms with a dull knife." Such action, if it happened, not only defied the etiquette of war, but bordered on barbarity. Geary himself had been associated with barbarity while serving as the territorial governor of "Bleeding Kansas" in 1857, where he had aligned with the abolitionists. It was not lost upon the Southerners that their enemy commander was the antislavery "Geary of Kansas notoriety." The Confederates also knew the date of the Bolivar Heights battle. October 16 marked the two year anniversary of the John Brown Raid during which four local citizens were killed.

Geary was not impressed. "This inhuman treatment incensed my troops exceedingly. . . . I fear its consequences may be shown in retaliatory acts hereafter."

Herr's Mill (center) became a ruin in the fall of 1861, torched by vengeful Confederates who deplored Herr's allegiance to the Union and his cooperation with Federal forces. (HFNHP)

45

1862
War's Wrinkled Front

Throughout the long, bleak winter of 1861, the fate of Harpers Ferry balanced in an "ill-boding lull." The place "presented a scene of the utmost desolation," remembered resident Joseph Barry. "All the inhabitants had fled, except a few old people, who ventured to remain and protect their homes, or who were unable or unwilling to leave the place." Most of the military presence had departed as well. A few companies of the 28th Pennsylvania Infantry patrolled the Potomac's Maryland shore as local companies of Ashby's cavalry continued vigilance on the Virginia side. Stonewall Jackson stationed himself at Winchester, too far away to concern himself with the Ferry. The river itself ultimately offered some respite from raids. Ashby reported on November 4 that the Potomac was flooding and had risen to its highest level since 1852, completely drowning the C&O Canal. Occasionally, some curious activity interrupted the boredom. Union military engineers were seen dashing back and forth across the river, taking notes and carrying surveying instruments. What did this mean?

Colonel Geary understood. Federal authorities had determined to rebuild the B&O Railroad bridge and to occupy and hold Harpers Ferry. Geary's mission was to scout the bridgehead and keep Washington apprised of Rebel obstructions to this plan. Geary thus sent intelligence sorties into Virginia, crossing at Harpers Ferry on a regular basis.

On February 7, 1862, George Rohr, a favorite scout of Geary's, spied an African American man along the Potomac shore waving a white flag. Both slaves and free blacks often

Primitive boats and skiffs became the principal method of access to the Ferry for Federal troops until repair of the railroad bridge in 1862. (LONDON ILLUSTRATED NEWS)

Top: The commercial heart of the town before being burned by Federal soldiers. (HFNHP)

Above: The officer commanding the torchbearers had his own ironic association with Harpers Ferry. Hector Tyndale, now a major in the 28th Pennsylvania Infantry, had escorted John Brown's wife to Harpers Ferry in December 1859. After Brown's execution, he escorted the widow and her husband's remains north. Just over two years later, Tyndale returned to burn that section of the town that fomented Brown's demise. (MASSACHUSETTS COMMANDERY MILITARY ORDER OF THE LOYAL LEGION/U.S. ARMY MILITARY HISTORY INSTITUTE)

proved good sources of intelligence for the Union, so Rohr and companions began rowing across the river, purportedly displaying their own flag. As they approached the Virginia shore, Confederates from Robert Baylor's cavalry company (concealed under the B&O trestle) opened fire. Rohr was killed. Reports soon circulated that Baylor had used his own slave, named John Sorrell, to lure Rohr with the intention of killing him. Baylor, who was not present, adamantly denied this charge. Colonel Geary awaited no explanation, and ordered his men to burn the buildings along the old railroad trestle and at the Point where "the Confederates were accustomed to conceal themselves and watch and annoy the Federal soldiers."

"Another calamity to the hapless town," wrote Joseph Barry, watching helplessly as the flames consumed all of the buildings between the armory entrance and ruins of the railroad bridge. The commercial heart of the town had been stabbed. The Wager Hotel, railroad station, water tower, and the Gault House Saloon—all made famous during the John Brown Raid—were destroyed.

Sacred Soil

*P*rior to Geary's burning of the Point, the Federals had been plotting a permanent presence in Harpers Ferry, determining that the town held strategic importance for the North. Located at the entrance into the Shenandoah Valley, the Ferry offered a launch pad for an invasion of Virginia. The B&O Railroad provided a line of transport and supply, and a Union force stationed at Harpers Ferry could protect its vital bridge crossing of the Potomac. The abandoned and partially destroyed armory buildings, immediately adjacent to the rails, could be repurposed as a depot ideal for the quartermaster and commissary departments. A Northern presence at Harpers Ferry could hinder a Confederate invasion of Maryland or Pennsylvania. A garrison at the Ferry could also protect Washington from potential enemy advances coming from north and west of the capital.

Major General George B. McClellan recognized the strategic importance of Harpers Ferry early in the war. Appointed President Lincoln's general-in-chief following the debacle of First Manassas, McClellan's grand plan for 1862 called for a Federal invasion and occupation of the Shenandoah Valley—thus protecting Washington's western flank—while the main army approached the enemy capital at Richmond. One significant barrier potentially thwarted McClellan's scheme: the Potomac River.

Sustaining an army in Virginia required a bridge across the Potomac. None now existed at Harpers Ferry. McClellan's solution was to first build a military span, followed by construction of a new railroad bridge. West Point trained engineers devised an innovative plan—build a bridge atop canal boats. They calculated 25 to 30 canal boats were necessary to span the 900-foot-wide river, and proposed that sea ships' anchors in Baltimore Harbor could be procured to make the bridge "very

General George B. McClellan adored his men, and they returned his adulation as the general watched them cross into the Confederacy, launching a diversionary invasion of the Shenandoah Valley in February 1862. (LOC)

stable and serviceable for all purposes." Better still, bridge builders of the B&O Railroad could perform the work in two days, and the boats could be floated up the canal, easing shipping difficulties. One issue remained: how do you remove the boats from the canal prism into the river? The solution: the original builders of the C&O Canal had installed a river outlet lock opposite Harpers Ferry.

General McClellan enthusiastically endorsed this plan. An alternative recommendation to utilize a bateaux bridge, comprised of smaller and lighter boats rather than the "clumsy canal boats," was dismissed. "To cross a river like the Potomac at this season," argued Chief Engineer John G. Barnard, "on an ordinary pontoon [bateaux] bridge, which may be swept away in 24 hours or less," was unacceptable. Thus, in the final week of February, mules began hauling canal boats up the C&O. Meanwhile, bateaux boats were on their way via rail for use as an initial, temporary span. "The pontoon train will serve best for the first crossing," declared General Nathaniel P. Banks, who commanded the invasion force. "It can be thrown across in a few hours, and we can transport artillery and supply wagons across by hand."

"I am able to report that the troops of this division are ready for immediate movement," General Banks informed McClellan on February 22, 1862. It was George Washington's 130th birthday. The United States he helped create was about to invade and occupy the Virginia he so deeply loved. As the Civil War neared its eleventh month, the holiday in honor of the Father of

Our Country was "observed by all classes of people here," noted General Banks from his headquarters at Frederick, Maryland. "Salutes were fired, and [Washington's Farewell] address was read to a very large concourse of soldiers and citizens. The services were impressive, and will produce an excellent effect."

Banks bestowed the honor of the first to step upon the "sacred soil" to the victors of Bolivar Heights—Colonel John W. Geary's command. Geary's soldiers, stationed in the Harpers Ferry area since last September, were familiar with the geography. The first assignment would be rigging a rope ferry across the Potomac, a craft Geary's men had perfected.

Just after daylight on February 24, the operation commenced. When the skiffs set out into the cold waters, the current rushed so swiftly that six soldiers drowned when their boats tipped. After several hours of struggle, the ferry was in place. Then nature turned against the Federals. "The weather, at first slightly perverse, became so exceedingly violent," recalled Geary. "The river rose so rapidly that it became dangerous to attempt to throw troops across." The storm raged all night, worrying the Yankees that delay would

Pontoon bridge across the Potomac River. (*Harper's Magazine*)

ruin the surprise and enable the Confederates to concentrate. The next morning was calm, with no Rebels on the shoreline. Geary methodically secured the bridge-head with eight companies of infantry and two cannon, fanning as far as Bolivar Heights. But Geary had one more river to conquer—the Shenandoah—as he also had a mission to seize Loudoun Heights, a lofty den for

Confederate sharpshooters. Undaunted, Geary's veterans paddled across the boulder-strewn Shenandoah and planted the Stars and Stripes atop Loudoun Heights. Garrisons were detached to the three blockhouse fortifications built nearly one year before by Jackson's Confederates. With the heights and town in Federal possession, the bridge builders commenced their work.

The C&O Canal Lock 33 opposite Harpers Ferry in the decade following the Civil War. The canal paralleled the Maryland bank of the Potomac River for 184.5 miles, stretching from Cumberland to Georgetown. (HFNHP)

General McClellan traveled out to watch the historic spectacle, making his headquarters at Sandy Hook in a large green passenger car loaned by the B&O Railroad. McClellan then ventured another mile upstream to witness the action. "The bridge was splendidly thrown [across]," McClellan reported, as he watched his military engineers piece together the erector set of bateaux, stringers, planking, and rope cable on February 26. "It was one of the most difficult operations of the kind ever performed."

For Charles Morse of the 2nd Massachusetts Infantry, who knew nothing about the art of pontoniers, "it was a beautiful bridge." Using his amateur eye, Morse described the structure. "At intervals of every twenty feet are the pontoons, which look like common flat bottom scows, and are

connected together by planking eight feet wide. The whole arrangement is connected to the shore by a system of ropes." Warren Lee Goss of the 9th New York Infantry noticed one "large rope-cable was stretched from shore to shore fifty feet above the bridge, and the upper ends of each boat was stayed to the cable by a smaller rope." Goss described the rushing river current bending the bridge "into a half-moon curve."

McClellan watched as his men marched across the bridge. Standing upon the stone coping of Lock 33 (just below the Maryland end of the pontoon bridge)—and surrounded by "his immense retinue of staff officers and orderlies"—McClellan's men had "an unobstructed view of him in passing." Edmund Brown of the 27th Indiana Infantry wrote, "This was the first time most of us had seen the then much adulated 'Little Mack.'"

Many soldiers were apprehensive as they approached the pontoon bridge. "Needless to say we had never seen one before," Brown noted. Most tramped across gingerly, as the bridge rocked and swayed and hardly felt stable. It was easy to lose balance—and a fall into the rapid river would lead to certain drowning. Since most of the men had never walked on a pontoon bridge, the army provided good guidance. "An officer stood at the end of the bridge and saw that the distances between the ranks were widened and the [marching] step broken," observed Brown. "The [horse and mule] teams, when the train came to cross, were detached from the wagons, and the latter were pushed over by hand. The same course was pursued by the artillery."

"The spirit of the troops is most excellent. They are in the mood to fight anything," McClellan apprised the Secretary of War. Edmund Brown of the 27th Indiana concurred. "This we regarded as an event of great importance. We were at last upon insurgent soil." Brown reasoned, "When the boundary of a state which had declared its separation from the Union was crossed, it was understood to mean that hostilities had begun."

For hours McClellan watched as 8,500 infantry, 18 cannon, and two squadrons of cavalry crossed into the Confederacy. "It is raining hard, but most of the troops are in [Harpers Ferry] houses," McClellan informed the Secretary of War late on the evening of February 26. With everything going exceedingly well, the commanding general concluded: "We will attempt the canal-boat bridge tomorrow."

The next day, however, the general faced a disparaging situation. No one in the United States Army had measured the width of the canal lock. Now they discovered the stone sluiceway was four inches too narrow for the canal boats to fit into the river lock. A maddened McClellan wrote to the Secretary of War, "It is impossible to construct the permanent bridge, as I intended." The ramifications were significant. "I cannot, as things now are, be sure of my supplies. . . . The wiser plan is to rebuild the railroad bridge as rapidly as possible, and then act according to the state of affairs." This episode proved an inauspicious beginning to the Union presence in the Shenandoah Valley.

"The murmur of many voices; the mellow, abrupt call of the Negro drivers to their mules; the glistening arms of the infantry; the dull rumble of artillery wheels and baggage wagons . . . live[d] in memory . . . as one of the pictures of 'war's wrinkled front.'"

—Private Warren Lee Goss, 9th New York Infantry

New Life

"Harpers Ferry was a fitting place to begin an advance against the rebellion," reflected the 27th Indiana's Edmund Brown. "It was a rebellion solely in the interests of slavery." As an exclamation to that point, Brown recalled regiment after regiment crossing the bridge, stepping upon Virginia soil for the first time, passing through the boat ramp ensconced in the armory river wall, and then seeing John Brown's Fort. Hundreds of voices sang, ringing the air with the melody: *John Brown's body lies a moldering in the grave, But his soul goes marching on.*

It was the second visit to Harpers Ferry for the 2nd Massachusetts Infantry. The previous summer, it had been the first U.S. regiment to enter the town. That visit ended with a retreat north. This time the army was advancing south and expected better results. "We found the place more wrecked and ruined

John Brown's Fort (center) inspired thousands of Union soldiers. A contraband camp can be seen in the foreground of this 1865 photo. (HFNHP)

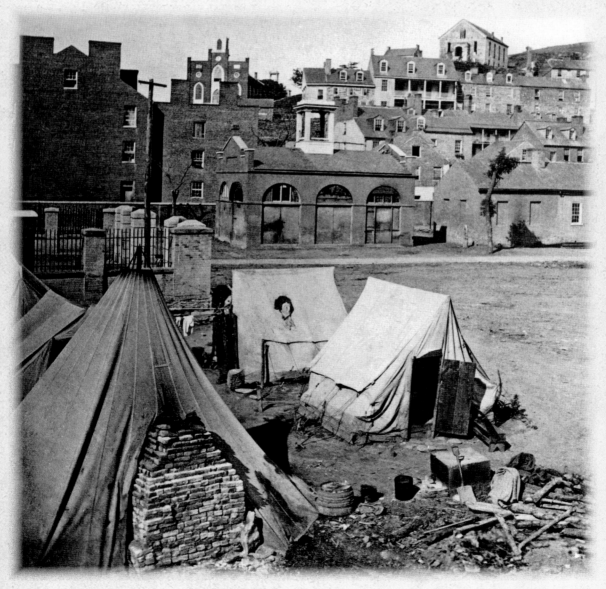

than when we last saw it," recollected Colonel George H. Gordon. "Blackened walls met the eye at every turn; there was no life in town. Now and then we saw a prowling inhabitant stealing around." Gordon's men promptly quartered in abandoned houses along Shenandoah Street, in which there was no shortage. Chaplain Alonzo Quint remembered, "We did not sleep on feather beds that night."

On the morning of February 28, McClellan's force moved toward Charles Town, with the general himself joining the cavalcade. His strategic goal was Winchester—the position of Stonewall Jackson. After completing his reconnaissance, the commanding general returned to his headquarters near Sandy Hook, and began his journey back to Washington to lead the main army toward Richmond. The Valley advance was left in the hands of General Banks.

Banks could proceed no further, however, without adequate supplies. McClellan subsequently instructed his subordinates to "use every exertion to establish as promptly as possible depots of forage and subsistence on the Virginia side" at Harpers Ferry. Abandoned armory buildings were identified for this purpose, and orders were given to ensure "the rapid transmission of supplies over the river." The Union army suffered from no lack of supplies—just its location along the Maryland shore. "The whole level bench between the mountain and the canal . . . was one mass of railway trains, engines, forage wagons, and mules," observed David Hunter Strother, now a Federal officer and scout. "Mountains of forage and commissary stores lay piled beside the trains; while groups of teamsters, negroes, quarter-masters' clerks, and train guards, cooking, sleeping, or dancing, huddled around the numerous fires that lighted this chaotic picture." All of it had to be moved to the opposite shore, without the benefit of the flawed and ill-fated permanent canal-boat bridge.

As supplies shuttled across the pontoon structure, Harpers Ferry came to life. Logistical support for an army of 20,000 required hundreds of

Top photos: *Soldiers from Baxter's Fire Zouaves (the 72nd Pennsylvania Infantry) bivouacked in buildings in Harpers Ferry in March 1862, and used their idle time to scrawl on walls. Wallpaper and layers of paint hid the graffiti on original plaster walls until discovered by National Park Service architects when restoring buildings in the 1980s.* (HFNHP)

Above: *The French Colonial Army operating in North Africa inspired the colorful Zouave uniform worn by a soldier from the Baxter's Zouaves.* (PHOTO COURTESY OF THE MILITARY AND HISTORICAL IMAGE BANK, WWW. HISTORICALIMAGEBANK.COM)

laborers in the rear. "The great number of soldiers who were stationed there [and] the many civilian strangers who daily arrived to visit friends in the army threw a new life into the town," recalled Joseph Barry. "Many of the old citizens returned to their homes, now comparatively safe, and accumulated snug fortunes in providing small luxuries for the wearied soldiers and their friends." Chaplain Quint of the 2nd Massachusetts also witnessed the rapid resuscitation. "Our soldiers were not in Harper's Ferry twenty hours before new signs were out—'military equipments,' 'salt fish, groceries, rum, and whiskey.'"

One of McClellan's primary purposes for occupying the Shenandoah Valley was the reconstruction and protection of the B&O line, nearly 80 miles of which ran through enemy territory. Bridge builders arrived one week after the Federals had secured Harpers Ferry, but because of the "great depth of water and the swiftness of the current, it was found impossible to raise the trestles." The workers persevered, however; and on March 18, 1862, the first locomotive in nine months chugged across the makeshift bridge into Harpers Ferry. The new utilitarian structure lacked the grandeur and craftsmanship of the previous wooden bridge, but it worked. The railroad soon was delivering tons of food, munitions, and clothing for storage within the grounds of the former musket factory. Further celebration ensued on March 29, when the entire line of the B&O reopened west to Cumberland.

The B&O Railroad rebuilt its Potomac River bridge shortly after the Federals reoccupied Harpers Ferry in early 1862. Stark iron trestling replaced the graceful wooden spans that adorned the antebellum bridge. (NARA)

Meeting the Enemy

Writer Nathaniel Hawthorne visited Harpers Ferry as a guest of the B&O Railroad's directors. "Harper's Ferry presents as striking a vista among the hills as a painter could desire to see," Hawthorne wrote. "But a beautiful landscape is a luxury, and luxuries are thrown away amid discomfort." The abandoned armory made an interesting topic for the famed author. "Piles of broken bricks and a waste of shapeless demolition, amid which we saw gun barrels in heaps of hundreds together." Hawthorne surmised "the brightest sunshine could not have made the scene cheerful, nor have taken away the gloom from the dilapidated town . . . it has an inexpressible forlornness."

Hawthorne had a particular curiosity about the John Brown Fort, but when he arrived at the building, he found it a jail for Confederate prisoners. "It was a wretched place," proclaimed Hawthorne, who suddenly found himself in the midst of 20 Rebels, several playing with "the dirtiest pack of cards I ever happened to see." As he studied and conversed with the captives, Hawthorne detected not "a trace of hostile feeling in the countenance, words, or manner of any prisoner there. Almost to a man they were simple, bumpkinlike fellows, dressed in homespun clothes, with faces singularly vacant of meaning, but sufficiently good-humored: a breed of men, in short, such as I did not suppose to exist in this country." Hawthorne left pontificating upon the "immense absurdity that they should fancy us their enemies."

Top: *Nathaniel Hawthorne* (LOC/PPOC); Above: Postwar photo of armory ruins. (HFNHP)

The Railroad Brigade

*J*ubilation raced through the Federal ranks two weeks after they had occupied Harpers Ferry. Outnumbered seven to one, Stonewall Jackson had evacuated Winchester without a fight, disappearing deep into the Shenandoah Valley. But Jackson's absence and the Federal jubilation was temporary. Jackson struck the Union rear at Kernstown on March 23. As General Banks kept a nervous eye on Jackson, General McClellan determined to fulfill his promise to protect the Baltimore and Ohio Railroad. On March 29, the same day the B&O reopened its line from Baltimore to Cumberland, McClellan ordered Colonel Dixon Stansbury Miles to report to Harpers Ferry to command the "Railroad Brigade."

Colonel Miles was a professional soldier. The 59-year-old native of Maryland had been in the army since he had entered West Point at age 15. His 42 years in the military—all of it in the infantry, except his student days at West Point—included the Mexican War, where he was brevetted three times for gallant and distinguished service. In recognition of his long and successful career, Miles ascended to the rank of full colonel—one of only 22 in the army—two years before the outbreak of Civil War. He outranked Robert E. Lee and other famous officers in the antebellum army. Unfortunately for Colonel Miles, his reputation was ruined at the Battle of First Manassas, where an army nemesis accused him of drunkenness while commanding the Union's reserve division. Although cleared of the charges, the damage was severe, and Miles was tarnished in the press. Dixon Miles became the scapegoat for the Union disaster at Manassas.

General McClellan, however, had confidence in Miles. Aware that the B&O Railroad was the umbilical cord for the Union army operating in the Shenandoah Valley, McClellan tasked Miles with an important assignment: protect all the rail lines between Washington and Baltimore; Harpers Ferry and Baltimore; Harpers Ferry west to the South Branch of the Potomac; and Harpers Ferry south to Winchester. This equaled some 380 miles—over half of that in the Confederacy. Undaunted, Miles established his headquarters at the former master armorer's house at the end of March and scattered his raw-recruit regiments to points deemed crucial along the rail lines.

It was a rocky start for Miles and his Railroad Brigade. On April 22, three weeks after Miles arrived, a Potomac flood destroyed the one-month old B&O bridge. "The bridge was covered with loaded coal cars last night to prevent the rising waters from carrying it off," observed John Mead Gould of the 10th Maine. It did not work. Gould watched as "a tree carried away one span and the cars on it hauled off those on the next span which lightened of its weight went off too. Afternoon a canal boat took away a third [span]

Colonel Dixon Stansbury Miles understood his purpose "to protect the Road from being torn up or bridges destroyed by Guerrillas." (LOC)

The B&O Railroad just west of Harpers Ferry. The Potomac River parallels the railroad on the left. Maryland Heights dominates the left horizon. Camp Hill towers to the right. Ruins of the armory appear in the middle distant. Telegraph poles stand wireless. Discarded rails—heated and bent by Confederates to make them useless—are scattered beside the repaired line. (NARA)

and at night a fourth went." Gould labeled the disaster a "nasty proceeding inasmuch as we have 500 barrels of one stuff or another on the Maryland side and nary an ounce of beef or bread here." Two weeks later on May 4, tireless B&O work crews completed another bridge—the third replacement in 10 months—and promptly "400 loaded cars passed over it." Just one month later on June 5, the Potomac rampaged yet again and once more the trestles could not withstand the current. The raging river not only interrupted railroad operations, but it also severed the cord between Miles and his supply route.

As the Potomac played havoc at Harpers Ferry, Miles turned his attention to his Confederate enemies, expeditiously deploying his initial force of

58

about 6,000 men to perform guard service at key railroad locations. He also prepared his command as a rapid deployment force that could move quickly to a trouble spot. Miles fully grasped that his Railroad Brigade did not exist "with the intention of fighting an army."

Stonewall Jackson changed that attitude with his abrupt and unexpected arrival in late May. Jackson had defeated General Banks' army in lightning strikes at Front Royal and Winchester. He then chased the Northerners across the Potomac at Williamsport, effectively eliminating all Yankee presence in the Shenandoah except at one location: Harpers Ferry. Jackson surged toward the Ferry, intending to clear the Valley of all the Union occupiers. Dixon Miles stood alone.

Concerned that a move against Harpers Ferry could threaten Washington, the Secretary of War rapidly rushed reinforcements to the Ferry via the B&O Railroad. It was the first tactical use of the B&O in the struggle for the Shenandoah Valley— using the rails to respond to a military emergency at the front. Brigadier General Rufus B. Saxton

Stonewall Jackson chased all the Federals out of the Shenandoah Valley at the outset of his famous Valley Campaign—except for the Yankees occupying Harpers Ferry. (NARA)

arrived on the morning of May 25. Saxton discovered only one Maryland infantry company at the Ferry. Miles had been ordered to move his force to Winchester to assist General Banks. General Saxton superceded Miles, and within 48 hours, as the troop transports kept rumbling in, Saxton's garrison had swelled to greater than 8,000 men—"raw troops, mostly new levies and militia regiments, turned out on the spur of the moment." Due to the inexperience of the men, Saxton reported: "Our movements are consequently slow." Washington was so desperate to stymie the emergency that it sent 300 sailors from the Washington Navy Yard to aid with Saxton's defenses. The sailors brought with them three heavy cannon, usually reserved for coastal forts, with one weighing nearly five tons. Saxton ordered the sailors

The Naval Battery (center) viewed here from Camp Hill and located in a tree clearing on Maryland Heights. (NARA)

to mount these guns on Maryland Heights—an extraordinary request considering the cannon weight and mountain height. As a precaution, Saxton also had the former slaves sheltered behind Union lines "at work moving the stores across the river."

As the troops and cannon arrived, Saxton deployed his soldiers across the Harpers Ferry peninsula. He crowned Bolivar Heights with most of his infantry and field artillery, stretching his line almost 2,000 yards from the Shenandoah to the Potomac, with hopes that its steep walls facing Jackson's approach would serve as a natural fortress. Two additional generals had arrived to command infantry. The sailors, meanwhile, had tugged the three naval cannon about one-third the way up Maryland Heights to an elevation that could support the men atop Bolivar Heights. Saxton sent a reconnaissance to Loudoun Heights, "where it was reported the enemy were in position." He was correct. A small Rebel force attacked the scouting party, but it rapidly dispersed when shells from the Naval Battery exploded on Loudoun Heights. Despite these dispositions, the Assistant Secretary of War who had arrived from Washington foresaw doom: "Regiments in a state of great demoralization, because of the terrible stories told by the runaways from Banks, who came straggling in." David Hunter Strother, who just had arrived at the Ferry, observed: "The excitement at Washington is said to be great. They refused to accept

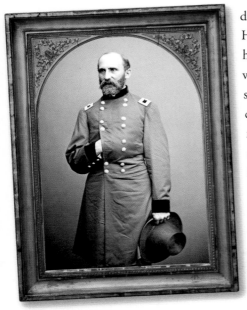

Brigadier General Rufus B. Saxton (LOC/PPOC)

the warnings of the coming storm, given in time to have averted it. Now they are on the other extreme, and have become alarmed."

Then Jackson appeared. "Clouds of dust were visible in various directions," Saxton ominously reported on May 28. Charles Town fell first to Stonewall, but then there was a mysterious lull. The next two days passed quietly. What was Jackson up to? General Saxton surmised Jackson's strategy. "It became evident that the enemy were seeking . . . to allure us from our strong defensive position [on Bolivar Heights] to one of their own selection." Saxton refused to take the Confederate bait. Jackson inched closer.

From his perch on Bolivar Heights, Strother watched the Rebels approaching, first to Halltown, then to School House Ridge. As the Southerners moved forward, they came within range of the Union cannon on Bolivar Heights. As the guns opened fire, Strother was unimpressed. "Artillerymen, guns, and all are quite new, and from unskillfulness or defective ammunition the firing was wretchedly bad." Knowing the enemy were experienced veterans, Strother watched with a mixture of humor and horror: "The shells burst midway in their flight—some immediately after leaving the muzzle of the gun; others tumbled into the fields without exploding. In case of an attack, our light artillery will be of little service, I fear."

Modern view from Bolivar Heights toward School House Ridge. Fewer trees existed at the time of Jackson's advance. (NPS)

Bolivar Heights and the village of Bolivar looking west from Camp Hill. Note the absence of trees along the ridge. (HFNHP)

Signs of Jackson's advance were visible by the late afternoon of May 29. Strother observed dust rising on the Harpers Ferry–Charles Town Turnpike, "indicating the advance of a large force." Just as troubling was the rising dust stretching toward the Potomac River and another dusty column shouldering the Shenandoah. Loudoun Heights was seized by the 2nd Virginia Infantry, the local regiment in the Stonewall Brigade. This signaled enemy flanking maneuvers along the rivers. On the night of May 29, General Saxton constricted his line by abandoning Bolivar Heights and moving his infantry to Camp Hill, a rounded knoll comprising the upper town of Harpers Ferry. This dramatically reduced the infantry defense, dwindling from 2,000 yards to 900 yards, enabling Saxton to shuffle soldiers to Maryland Heights to protect the Naval Battery and guard against a Confederate move north of the Potomac.

The nighttime crossing of the river into Maryland proved a harrowing adventure. "There was a rope ferry, with a single scow, requiring an hour at least to cross, discharge, and return," Strother reported. To provide a more efficient passageway, the single-track railroad bridge was

"In front of each regiment was a chaplain gesticulating and praying at the top of his voice. . . . I cannot say that I was favorably impressed with the exhibition. Perhaps a double jigger of whiskey and a sharp military appeal would have been better calculated to make the men stand up to their work."
—**David Hunter Strother**

floored with planking about eight feet wide. But it was more frightening than the ferry. Forty feet above the river, this walkway had no handrails. Soldiers, horses, wagons, and cannon had to trek nearly 1,000 feet—in after midnight darkness—across the bridge. Two by two the infantry marched across. The artillerymen pushed and pulled their guns. Cavalrymen, in single file, led their horses. "Several horses got frightened and leaped over into the water," Strother recalled. One crashed upon an old railroad engine rusting in the river and instantly was killed. "Strange to say, the others, striking deep water, swam ashore and were saved."

All the bluecoats anticipated a battle for Bolivar Heights on Friday, May 30, but Jackson only teased the Federals with some skirmishing from afar. Strother admitted he was "profoundly mystified. . . . Jackson seems to have deliberately set about investing this place . . . but he has been dawdling around for several days, and has made no serious attempt yet." When Strother scaled Maryland Heights to view the situation from the Naval Battery, he discovered a probable reason. "Should the enemy attempt to cross [Bolivar Heights] he will be swept by shell and shrapnel from this battery." Strother also was impressed with the Camp Hill infantry line, then being entrenched, from which a scathing musketry fire could be delivered. "I feel some confidence that Jackson will smell brimstone if he attempts Harper's Ferry at this time."

Strother guessed wrong. In a fierce thunderstorm just before dusk, the Confederates rushed Bolivar Heights with infantry, cavalry, and artillery. The Naval Battery and the Union infantry on Camp Hill responded with ferocity. Saxton marveled at the pyrotechnics. "The rains descended in torrents; vivid flashes of lightning illuminated at intervals the grand and magnificent scenery, while the crash of thunder, echoing among the mountains, drowned into comparative insignificance the roar of our artillery." The Confederates pushed down Bolivar Heights and through the town of Bolivar, coming within 300 yards of the Federal defense on Camp Hill. There they halted. By the next day, the Rebels had vanished. Jackson had raced southward to avoid entrapment from Union columns attempting to close his escape 50 miles up the Valley. Harpers Ferry was secure.

"The thanks of this Department are cordially tendered to you for your late able and gallant defense of Harper's Ferry," stated the commendation to General Saxton from the grateful Secretary of War. "You were placed in command at that point at a moment of extreme danger and under circumstances of extraordinary difficulty. By your gallantry and skill great service was rendered to the country." Saxton departed Harpers Ferry on June 2, never to return. The same could not be said about Stonewall Jackson.

Martial Law

Remaining behind, and once again assuming command of the Railroad Brigade, was Colonel Dixon Miles. Miles served as Saxton's chief of staff during the Stonewall scare. Saxton proved a good mentor, and as a careful student, Miles witnessed every Saxton decision and experienced the happy and fruitful results. Little could Miles predict that in the not-too-distant future, he would find it necessary to call upon these pleasant memories in his own unpleasant situation.

With the Confederate emergency abated, Miles turned his attention to the more mundane matters of military life. For four consecutive days, summer monsoons had drenched the Shenandoah and Potomac Valleys and the Allegheny Highlands. Miles knew the confluence of the two rivers would exacerbate the current. Would the railroad bridge withstand the deluge? On June 5, Miles reported "the flood has damaged us greatly; swept the bridge entirely off, except the west span." The flood waters also immersed storehouses, the depot arsenal, and stables. Fortunately Miles had time to evacuate their contents. The military brass, convinced that a pontoon bridge was needed at the Ferry at all times to ensure connection with the Maryland shore, ordered bridge parts and the pontoon was operational by August. Meanwhile, Miles ordered a steam tug "which will answer our purpose to pass stores over the river."

Rebuilding and guarding the Winchester and Potomac Railroad became another mission of Miles. Opening in the mid-1830s, the W&P was the first successful railroad in Virginia, extending 28 miles between Harpers Ferry and Winchester (the Valley's largest town). Stonewall's Confederates had wrecked the line during their May incursion; but the Union military contracted with the B&O builders to have the railroad reopened, and by the third week of June, "little grasshopper engines" were chugging up and down the line. The Federals reestablished their garrison post at Winchester, and the W&P once again operated as the supply line. Miles scattered his infantry along the route to protect bridges, trestles, and depots from Confederate guerillas.

Colonel Miles used this broadside, about the size of a poster, to announce General Order No. 18. (HFNHP)

Predicting the railroads, especially the Winchester line, "will be torn up" without more guards, Miles requested an experienced infantry regiment for the task. "It is worse than useless to put raw and undisciplined troops on the railroad," argued Miles. "It requires the best." The War Department adversely offered the colonel a newly organized *cavalry* regiment, *without any horses or firearms.*

Frustrated by Washington's response, Miles assigned the horseless riders to artillery duty on Maryland Heights—manning the monstrous guns at the Naval Battery just vacated by the sailors. "Being dissatisfied at not being mounted," Colonel Miles found the 600 troopers of the 8th New York Cavalry in a "disorganized and mutinous condition." The humorless regular army infantry colonel had the perfect solution: make them foot soldiers. Colonel Miles "tried to get us to take muskets and act as infantry," recorded Henry Norton of the 8th New York, "but as the men had enlisted for cavalry they refused to take them." Miles eventually convinced the cavalrymen to garner muskets, but Norton explained, "they had been stacked in front of our quarters for weeks, and rained full, which made them useless." Miles then armed the companies with antiquated Hall's carbines (once produced at Harpers Ferry and out of date for at least 20 years) and assigned them to guard duty on the W&P Railroad. "We refused to move as infantry," Norton scoffed. Exasperated, Miles informed his department chief: "These men will do no work, nor . . . anything else, not having horses nor arms." Little could Miles imagine that the 8th New York Cavalry soon would be on a rescue mission on his behalf.

"Take no prisoners and utterly destroy the town or houses near where Guerillas do their damage. . . . I have given this notice to the people, that those will be my orders, so soon as such a warfare was attempted. I would spare nothing life or property."

—**Colonel Dixon S. Miles**

The 8th New York eventually relented to the demands of Colonel Miles, but only if he promised good food and a good guard location nearby Harpers Ferry. The regiment commenced watch at Halltown, the first village along the W&P four miles south of the Ferry. Miles' concern for the safety of the railroad was real. Elements of Ashby's cavalry were on the prowl, especially Company B, 12th Virginia Cavalry, comprised of Jefferson County locals who were operating "in the land of our childhood and the beloved home of our riper years." These Rebels proved a constant irritant to Miles, with the railroad their favorite target. Once they captured a mail train carrying important military dispatches. They robbed a Federal paymaster of $4,000 in greenbacks intended to pay U.S. troops. They burned train cars and ruined one engine; its furnace heated "ten times hotter than it was wont to be." They ripped down telegraph lines and tore up tracks. Miles considered these raiders criminals and guerillas, and he believed the region "infested" with them.

Miles also made daily existence miserable for local citizens who refused to take the "Oath of Allegiance" to the United States government. "Every man, woman or boy of sixteen or over and residing in the Town of Harper's Ferry and Bolivar should subscribe to the Oath of Allegiance, or remove beyond the lines of our army . . . and if they return, to be treated as spies." The stifling martial law enacted by Colonel Miles extended to the daily meals of local residents. After implementing stringent controls on the purchase or trade of food—even for citizens loyal to the Union—Miles explained he was "anxious that the honest inhabitants should not be inconvenienced or distressed." For those who refused to take or abide by the Oath, Miles warned that he had "not the remotest idea of permitting rebellious traitors being fed, and pampered, to invigorate their traitorous designs, to the injury and prejudice of the Republic."

Summer Soldiers

A New York studio photographer arrived in Harpers Ferry in August 1862, recording nearly 200 images of the 22nd New York State Militia. Below: A company parades on Camp Hill, with the Odd Fellows' Lodge (still standing today) visible to the left. (NARA) Bottom: The camp of the 22nd NYSM on Camp Hill in August 1862. The imposing mansion in the background is the former quarters of the armory superintendent. (HFNHP) Opposite page, top: A company forms along Fillmore Street (foreground) on Camp Hill. St. John's Lutheran Church, little altered today from its wartime appearance, stands just to the left of center along Washington Street. The tents in the left background are on Bolivar Heights. (NARA) Opposite page, middle: Company E at rest on Camp Hill. (LOC/PPOC)

Assisting Colonel Miles with the implementation of his edicts were soldiers like those in the 22nd New York State Militia. As a state National Guard organization, the men had to serve only 90 days of active duty. The regiment, comprised of just over 600 volunteers, arrived at Harpers Ferry from New York City during the third week of June. It soon established its presence on Camp Hill, where the men were quartered in empty houses. "Of these there were plenty," recalled the regimental historian. "So many, in fact, that two were torn down and ten gutted for wood for the regimental campfires." Once the tents arrived, they were pitched in company street alignment on the grounds of the abandoned armory superintendent's quarters. The regimental chronicler remembered that "the doors of many [houses] were carried to camp and used to sleep on."

Many of the civilian martial law controls also pertained to the military occupiers. "No one was permitted to be out after dark," reported the 22nd New York State Militia historian, "and no soldier at any time, without a pass, which had to be shown to all guards and pickets. All lights were required to be extinguished at 9 p.m." He also deemed it curious that "white civilian travel was conspicuous by its absence."

Since Colonel Miles had no major Confederate army operating in his sector, he determined to drill his regiments to improve their combat preparation. The 22nd New York drilled daily (except Sunday) for about six hours. Company drill started each morning, followed by either three afternoons of battalion drill or three afternoons of brigade drill. Most of the drilling occurred on Bolivar Heights, "where there was plenty of

Soldiers of the 22nd NYSM and a replica of their knapsack and bedroll. (LOC/PPOC; HFNHP, NPS, Photographer Marsha Wassel)

room, but where the rough and broken ground made it hard work." Colonel Miles was "a splendid drill officer, with a peculiarly penetrating voice that would carry the entire length of the line of 2,500 men." Temperatures often soared to near 100 degrees, "like the heat of a baker's oven." The men marched to and from the drill grounds on roads filled with three inches of dirt. Dust clouds were often so thick that it was "impossible to see the length of a company or to tell whether the column consisted of 600 men or 600 cattle." Every day following drill, the soldiers headed for the

C&O Canal to remove the dust and grime. The canal "presented a singular sight" as it filled with up to 2,000 "naked men, laughing, shouting and swimming races."

Water for swimming and bathing was ample at Harpers Ferry, but good drinking water for thousands of soldiers presented a serious problem. "The spring water was so impregnated with lime that it looked like milk, and acted like a cathartic," recalled one soldier. For men in the 22nd New York, diarrhea became so universal that "all drills had to be stopped for a week, and there were not enough men fit for duty in the regiment to supply the camp guard." An innovative prescription for this problem was issuing a daily ounce of whiskey to each man, who mixed it with the water in his canteen, with a prohibition of drinking any other water.

The Matron

*D*ue to the prevalence of illness and a mid-summer evacuation of wounded and sick from vulnerable Winchester, a base hospital was established upon Camp Hill in the former paymaster's quarters—a stately brick mansion overlooking the picturesque water gap and the town cemetery. By the third week of July, "Clayton General Hospital" housed 285 patients. "Long and open tents are pitched in the [adjoining] yard which are generally preferred by the invalids to the hospital proper," reported a *New York Times* correspondent. "Several of the patients have been wheeled out upon the large balcony, projecting from the second story, where they sit enjoying the beautiful scene and the balmy atmosphere."

Mrs. Abba A. Goddard, "Matron of the General Hospital," had little time to yield to pleasantries. Her job was to make the hospital as comfort-

Clayton General Hospital
Many Union soldiers stationed at Harpers Ferry suffered from illness. They convalesced here, once the home of the armory paymaster, where the large balcony porch, beautiful views, and commodious rooms aided with recovery. (NPS, Photographer Marsha Wassel)

able as possible—a difficult task as the government provided minimal medical service and limited comforts for the infirm. Matron Goddard, who had traveled to Dixie to care for the lads of her hometown 10th Maine Regiment, depended upon donated money and charity boxes from friends and families from Portland and the "down east" region. "It is useless to attempt to describe the feeling experienced when one

of our boys comes in for a share of home charity," Mrs. Goddard penned in a letter home to the Portland newspaper. "I can say, yes comrade, your mother, your sister, your wife helped supply these comforts; enjoy them and welcome!" Within two weeks of her arrival at the Ferry, Matron Goddard had received 17 boxes filled with slippers, socks, fans, pin cushions, towels, pocket-handkerchiefs and checkerboards. She also received a hefty $150 contribution. In comparison, a private made $13 a month.

Once a week Mrs. Goddard traveled by train to Baltimore to purchase articles that could not be procured anywhere else. She departed Harpers Ferry at 3:00 a.m., arrived in Baltimore at 7:00 a.m., and then visited the markets—buying in volume single barrels of potatoes, onions, ginger cakes, Boston crackers, soda crackers, cornmeal, a box of lemons, and 100 pounds of codfish. Goddard returned to the Ferry by 6:00 p.m. laden with her shopping, and often "served up some of these same articles at the meals [the same] day." Mrs. Goddard proclaimed to her patrons, "It is no vanity in me to say that [through] the efforts of the last month the very lives of many of our men have been preserved."

Matron Goddard was so proficient in acquiring wholesome food that the head surgeon of the hospital, Dr. Ezekiel Dawson, placed her in charge of the entire cooking department for the sick. "You are authorized to furnish vegetables, condiments, and fruits," Dawson instructed. He asked Goddard to "prepare the diet, and to institute whatever regulations you deem necessary for the equitable distribution thereof." Dawson promised help in preparing tables and dining rooms and cleaning dishes. He also guaranteed Goddard "female help in [former slave] contraband cooks." Goddard took pride in her assignment and her perseverance. "I live on the warm side of a six-horse-power cook stove, kept at roasting point, from 5 a.m. until 7 p.m.," she explained. Recalling her cool weather home in Maine, she proclaimed: "I try to sleep in a room just over the same cook stove nightly, and meanwhile the thermometer stands 96 in the shade."

One of Matron Goddard's happiest moments occurred over a *Bible* she had picked up as a souvenir from the

The Civil War was the first American war where women provided substantial relief to thousands of sick and wounded soldiers. (HARPER'S WEEKLY)

THE SISTER OF CHARITY

May Bolivar Heights battle. While discussing her find a sick man suddenly yelled: "What name did you say?" The soldier burst into tears, exclaiming: "Oh my mother. It was her *Bible* and I lost it that day!" Mrs. Goddard watched Erastus Dibble of the 78th New York Infantry kiss the book upon its return, "baptizing it with the tears of filial affection."

The future of other convalescents worried the Matron. "When I look at our host of maimed—some without an arm, some without a leg, others minus a foot—and realize their privation is life-long . . . I can hardly restrain my tears." Melancholy about their prospects, Goddard wrote: "Soon they will be discharged from the service, and return to their homes; and I wonder what will become of them? We shall soon have such a company of cripples in our cities and towns [and] I am afraid will grow familiar, and individual sympathy be wanting." These marble men made Goddard scorn the "weak-backed coward sneaks, who became suddenly afflicted with crick-in-the-back, pain-to-the-stomach, weakness-in-the-knees, etc."

As the summer melted into September, Mrs. Goddard's hospital was closed and the patients moved to Frederick. "The cause of this sudden removal is a mystery," she reported. "I am informed that some important events are about to transpire, but I am not permitted to tell—because I don't know what they are." Matron Goddard did notice increased firing from the Naval Battery. She also received reports about a series of annoying "surprises." Seventeen Union pickets were surprised and captured while picking blueberries nearby; guards on a Winchester & Potomac train had been surprised, the passengers robbed, and the cars destroyed. On September 2, a cavalry reconnaissance of 300 men was surprised at Leesburg and reportedly annihilated. That same night about 10:30 p.m., a screeching shell from the Naval Battery flew overhead and awakened Mrs. Goddard. "Keen eyes have discovered an enemy," she declared. "There is no more sleep in this town tonight." The next morning she learned that the cannon was firing at the Leesburg cavalry returning from its mission. "I want a commission, and desire a company of women too old, and too familiar with the world, to be easily surprised by anybody or anything. With such a squad the valley of the Shenandoah would be perfectly safe." Actually, the Valley was very unsafe.

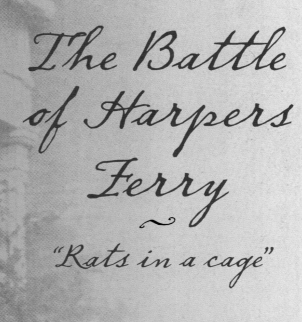

The Battle of Harpers Ferry

"Rats in a cage"

A foreboding shadow cast toward Harpers Ferry in the late summer of 1862. General Robert E. Lee's Confederate army was no longer defending Richmond. After a string of Union defeats, Lee now threatened Washington. Winchester was hastily evacuated the first week of September. Picket duty at Harpers Ferry was serious business now. Colonel Miles demanded that all avenues of approach be secured. No one was permitted to enter or leave Harpers Ferry without a pass. Tension mounted.

The pickets, however, almost universally made exception when approached by fleeing slaves. This phenomenon had occurred with frequency during the summer of 1862. As the Union army occupied the Shenandoah Valley, hundreds of slaves ventured north, seeking refuge behind the Federal lines at Harpers Ferry. "Poor bedraggled, foot-sore wretches" would suddenly appear in front of a Federal picket "in the gray of the morning, having walked ten or fifteen miles during the night—frequently a woman, carrying a baby, and with little children clinging to her skirts. The men carried their few

While in Harpers Ferry photographing the 22nd New York State Militia, a photographer took this image of a group of contraband posed at the main entrance of the former armory superintendent's residence on Camp Hill. The fate of these former slaves would be determined by the outcome of General Lee's first invasion of the North. (HFNHP)

75

possessions in a big bundle, tied to a stick, and the women usually 'toted' a roll of bedding." The regimental historian of the 22nd New York State Militia estimated 5,000 runaway slaves had crowded into Harpers Ferry during the hot, dry summer of 1862. "How they lived was a mystery," he recorded. "They crowded the empty houses, and overran the camp, washing clothes, selling pastry, berries and similar articles, and doing odd jobs. . . . Nearly every mess, and many of the men, had a servant who was glad to do anything for something to eat, or for a small quantity of loose change."

Colonel Miles made use of the "contraband" (the formal government designation for the enslaved seeking freedom behind Union lines), impressing them to construct an earthwork fortification on Camp Hill. The fortification extended from the bluffs of the Shenandoah and Potomac, across the western crest of Camp Hill. It traversed the grounds of the former armory superintendent's house, and appeared as a parapet six feet high, boasting a nine-foot by four-foot dry ditch along its western slope. Twenty pieces of various-sized artillery eventually occupied this position, with most of their cannon muzzles facing toward Bolivar Heights. Colonel Miles would soon be employing those cannon in the fight of his life.

At the end of August, Robert E. Lee's Army of Northern Virginia had defeated the Federals at the Battle of Second Manassas. Lee immediately followed this victory with a Confederate invasion into Maryland. With the Rebels in possession of Frederick—only 20 miles distant from Harpers Ferry—the eyes of both North and South focused upon Dixon Stansbury Miles and Harpers Ferry.

Lee's intentions were unknown. On September 5, Miles received an adamant directive from Major General John E. Wool in Baltimore: "Be energetic and active, and defend all places to the last extremity. . . . There must be no abandoning of post, and shoot the first man that thinks of it."

President Lincoln's General-in-Chief concurred, ordering Miles to stand fast. "Our army in motion," wired Major General Henry W. Halleck on September 7. "It is important that Harper's Ferry be held to the latest moment. The Government has the utmost confidence in you, and is ready to give you full credit for the defense it expects you to make."

"Thanks for the confidence," Miles replied. "Will do my best." Then the telegraph went silent. The wires had been cut by the invading Confederates, leaving Colonel Miles isolated and alone.

Back in Frederick, Lee faced an unexpected problem: 14,000 Union soldiers at Harpers Ferry and Martinsburg threatened his avenue of supply and

"You will not abandon Harper's Ferry without defending it to the last extremity."
—**John E. Wool, September 5, 1862**

Major General John E. Wool
(LOC)

In the Service of Uncle Sam

The War Between the States produced many phenomena, including human contraband. As Shenandoah Valley native David Hunter Strother described it: "Society was thrown into a ferment by the advent of a wagonload of negroes." The entourage, composed of several families, "with their household goods and plunder, [were] en route for a free country." The steady migration of fleeing slaves produced a quandary for General Nathaniel Banks. Early in the war, the official position of the United States government was not to interfere with slavery. The cause of war was "National Unity," and that alone. Military policy regulated that escaped slaves were jailed and returned to their owners. "But the sight of this family of emigrants, with its household goods and gods," Strother reasoned, "could not be misunderstood." Thus General Banks devised a solution. "Without any authority or wish to return them to their owners," the Massachusetts politician sent them to Harpers Ferry to assist the quarter master in loading and unloading army stores. Strother agreed this "seemed to afford a solution to the difficulty." The fleeing families were marched in squads to the Ferry and set to work, "earning their bread and beans in Uncle Sam's service."

CONTRABANDS COMING INTO THE FEDERAL CAMP IN VIRGINIA.
from a sketch by Edwin Forbes

Hundreds of enslaved people escaped their bondage and sought refuge behind Federal lines at Harpers Ferry, beginning with the first U.S. occupation in 1861. Many of these "contraband of war" earned their first wages cooking and washing clothes for Union soldiers. (THE SOLDIER IN OUR CIVIL WAR, 1885, FRANK LESLIE)

communication in the Shenandoah Valley. "I have no doubt they will leave that section," Lee confidently predicted to President Jefferson Davis on September 5. Four days later, Lee was disappointed to learn not one bluecoat had departed the Valley.

Frustrated by the Union army's failure to cooperate, Lee turned his full attention toward Harpers Ferry. Further delay in opening his supply route was intolerable. The Federals holding the Valley had to be removed or eradicated. Harpers Ferry—never intended as a target in Lee's first invasion—suddenly became *the* target.

To eliminate the Harpers Ferry nuisance, Lee developed a plan labeled Special Orders 191. He would divide his army into four columns. Three would converge upon Harpers Ferry and seize the three mountains surrounding the town. The fourth column would move 15 miles northwest to Boonsboro, where it would await the return of the Harpers Ferry expedition. Although splitting and scattering his army, the Confederate commander anticipated minimal danger from the enemy. The Federals had been acting defensively since the invasion of Maryland, spreading and covering all approaches to Washington and Baltimore. Lee expected his foe to remain cautious and nonaggressive, permitting ample time for his army to complete the Harpers Ferry operation and reunite.

To execute the Harpers Ferry operation, Lee selected Stonewall Jackson, a general with vast experience in the area. During his tenure as commandant of the post in the spring of 1861, Jackson had analyzed and memorized the Harpers Ferry terrain. Pleased at the prospect of returning to his beloved Shenandoah Valley, Jackson observed that he had been neglecting his friends there for some time. Lee replied that some of those "friends" probably would *not* be happy to see Stonewall.

Six of Lee's nine infantry divisions were assigned to the Harpers Ferry mission. On the morning of September 10, two-thirds of the Rebel army, approximately 28,000 men, departed Frederick and headed toward the Ferry.

Stonewall Jackson faced a complex challenge. His three diverging columns approached Harpers Ferry from three different directions, with three separate mountaintops as his objectives. Geography complicated the plan further. Two of the columns had to recross the Potomac River into Virginia without bridges or pontoons. In addition, Jackson's wing had to scale two mountains (Catoctin and South Mountain) en route to the river. Upon reaching Harpers Ferry, the Potomac and Shenandoah Rivers could hamper communications between the Confederates. Special Orders 191 required an extraordinary level of coordination and communication. Would it work?

General Robert E. Lee expected the Union forces to abandon Harpers Ferry and the Shenandoah Valley when he commenced his invasion of Maryland. When the Federals refused to yield—threatening Lee's rear and his line of supply—he devised a plan to destroy or capture the enemy based at the Ferry. (LOC/PPOC)

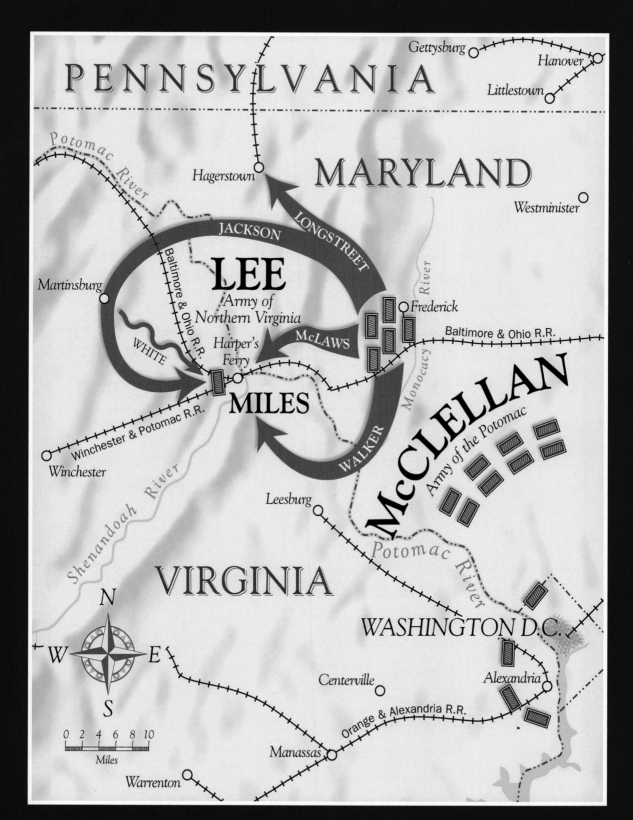

General Lee sent two-thirds of the Confederate army to invest Harpers Ferry to ensure no avenues of escape. Special Orders 191 instructed three separate columns to converge and seize the three mountains surrounding the Ferry, trapping the Federals in a natural hole. (MAP BY GENE THORP © 2000)

79

(Confidential)

Hd Qrs Army of Northern Va
Sept 9th 1862

Special Orders)
   No 191   )

III   The army will resume
its march to-morrow taking the Hagerstown road Gen Jacksons Command
will form the advance and after
passing Middletown with such portion
as he may select take the route towards
Sharpsburg. cross the Potomac at the
most convenient point & by Friday
Morning take possession of the
Baltimore & Ohio R.R. capture such
of the Enemy as may be at Martinsburg
and intercept such as may attempt
to Escape from Harpers Ferry

IV   Gen Longstreets command will
pursue the main road as far as Boonsboro when it will halt, with reserve supply
na baggage trains of the army

V   Gen McLaws with his own
division and that of Gen R.H. Anderson
will follow Gen Longstreet. on reaching
Middletown will take the route to
Harpers Ferry and by Friday Morning
possess himself of the Maryland
Heights and Endeavor to capture the
Enemy at Harpers Ferry and vicinity
VI   Gen Walker with his division

General Lee's instructions for the investment of Harpers Ferry mysteriously fell into the hands of the enemy commander. (Courtesy of the North Carolina State Archives and History, Raleigh, North Carolina)

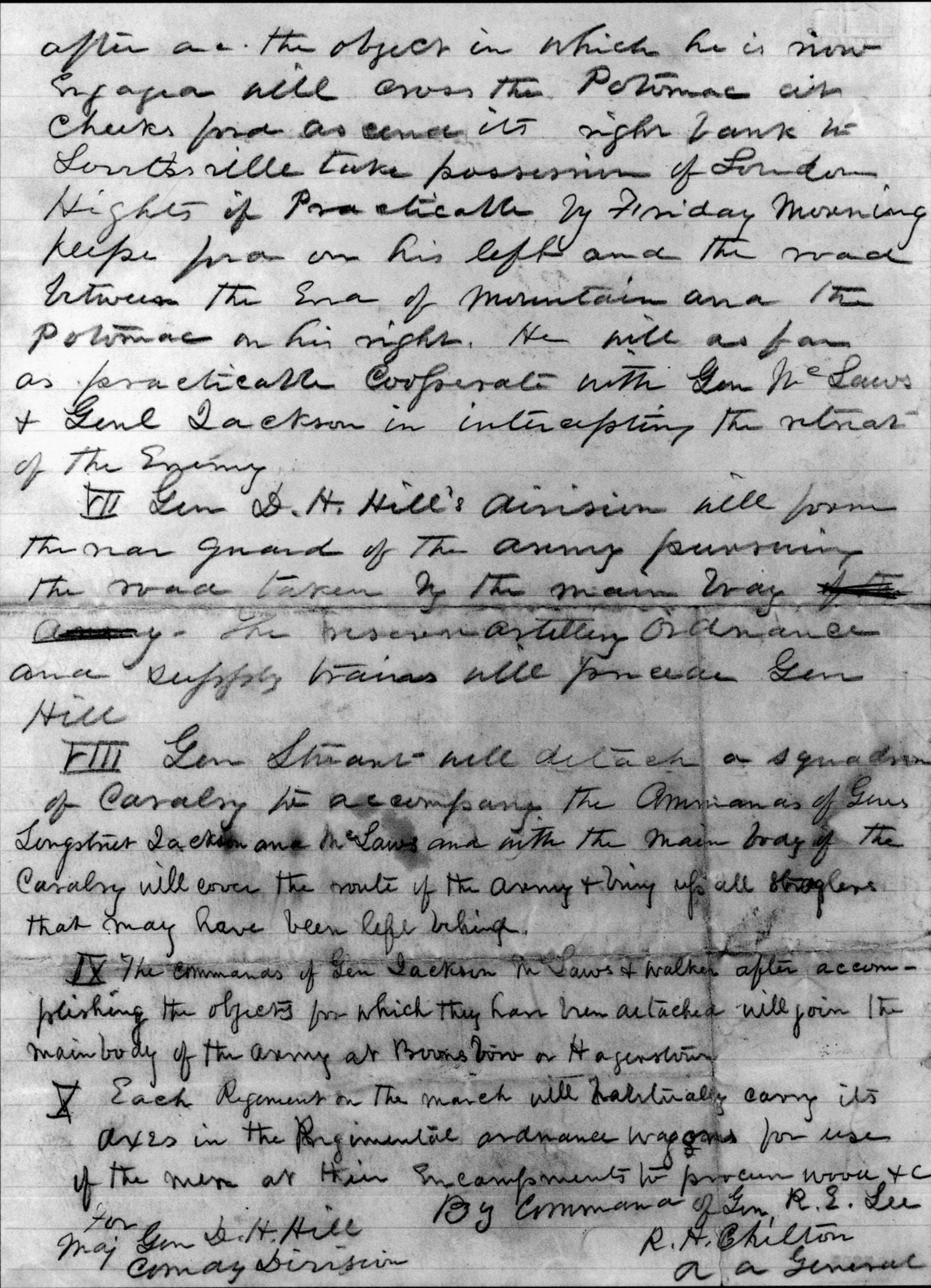

after a.c. the object in which he is now engaged will cross the Potomac at Cheeks ford ascend its right bank to Lovettsville take possession of London Hights if Practicable By Friday Morning Keyes [Keys] ford on his left and the road between the End of Mountain and the Potomac on his right. He will as far as practicable Cooperate with Gen McLaws & Genl Jackson in intercepting the retreat of the Enemy.

VII Gen D. H. Hill's division will form the rear guard of the army pursuing the road taken by the main body. The Reserve artillery Ordnance and supply trains will precede Gen Hill

VIII Gen Stuart will detach a squadron of Cavalry to accompany the commands of Genl Longstreet Jackson and McLaws and with the main body of the Cavalry will cover the route of the army & bring up all stragglers that may have been left behind.

IX The commands of Gen Jackson McLaws & Walker after accomplishing the objects for which they have been detached will join the main body of the army at Boonsboro or Hagerstown

X Each Regiment on The march will habitually carry its axes in the Regimental ordnance waggons for use of the men at their Encampments to procure wood &c

By Command of Gen R. E. Lee

For Maj Gen D. H. Hill
Comdg Division

R. H. Chilton
A. A. General

Add to these complications the presence of Colonel Miles and his garrison. The Confederates were baffled that the Northerners had not withdrawn, indicating a prospect for battle. Colonel Miles knew the Confederates were concentrating against him, as his cavalry reported regularly on the Rebel movements. Recalling his experience with General Saxton back in May, Miles determined to model his defense in a similar manner. This time, however, there were major differences. Jackson had 28,000 soldiers this time—ten times more than in May. The remainder of the Confederate army was within a day's march, unlike in May, when the main Rebel army was 150 miles away defending Richmond. Jackson also held advantage in position, as the Confederates were already north of the Potomac in Maryland. Lee's invasion had separated Miles from Washington. The Confederates also had possession of the B&O Railroad, eliminating the possibility of rushing reinforcements to the front. One other threat to Colonel Miles—Jackson outnumbered him two to one.

Regardless of odds, Miles prepared for a fight. He knew that Maryland Heights must be held. From his May experience, he remembered the long-range guns at the Naval Battery could support infantry on Bolivar Heights—a ridge crucial to defend against attackers approaching from the Shenandoah Valley. He added cannon behind the earthworks on Camp Hill to add more protection for Bolivar Heights. That left only Loudoun Heights undefended. Miles determined to leave it unoccupied, just as Saxton had done in May. He reasoned this mountain presented no threat so long as the Union forces commanded the superior high ground on Maryland Heights. Miles also considered Loudoun Heights too distant for infantry fire and too rugged for transport of artillery. He believed he could sacrifice Loudoun Heights, but he must hold elsewhere.

Despite his deployments, Miles was worried. How well would his troops fight? Most of his men had never been in battle. Many of his soldiers had been in the army for less than one month. The week before the Confederate invasion, four raw New York regiments had reported to Colonel Miles' headquarters. The 115th and 126th had been in the army but six days. The 111th Infantry had worn its blue uniforms for only one week. The 125th Regiment arrived just three days after mustering. Miles protested that his command was becoming nothing more than "a fortified camp of instruction." Just before the Confederate invasion, Miles fumed in a letter to General Wool: "The general states he has sent me two strong regiments. I have received but one, and the men belonging to it never had a gun in their hands until the boxes were opened and muskets issued to them yesterday; nor does an officer of the command . . . know how to drill or anything about the drill." As the Confederates approached, the time for drill had passed.

The Battle for Harpers Ferry

*T*hree days after departing Frederick, the Confederate columns converged upon the Ferry. Encountering no resistance on Loudoun Heights, Major General John G. Walker's division of nearly 4,000 men planted the Rebel flag on September 13. By noon, Jackson's 15,000 men in three divisions seized School House Ridge, effectively sealing any Federal escape via the Shenandoah Valley.

Now all eyes turned upon Maryland Heights—the key to the defense or capture of Harpers Ferry. Throughout the day, Mississippi and South Carolina Confederates under Major General Lafayette McLaws waged a fierce fight over and through a bolder-strewn thicket on a narrow crest, stoutly defended by the Federals. The Unionists conducted "a most obstinate and determined resistance" for almost nine hours. Inexplicably, about 3:30 p.m., Colonel Thomas Ford, the Federal commander on Maryland Heights who was not standing upon the ridge top but way down slope at the Naval Battery, ordered the mountain abandoned. "God Almighty!" screamed Colonel Dixon Miles, wheeling his horse toward the Union retreat from his command post on Bolivar Heights. "What does that mean? They are coming down! Hell and damnation!"

The loss of Maryland Heights did not portend good tidings for the Federals. With Miles sealed on the peninsula south of the Potomac, Jackson's noose tightened. Yet Miles refused to wave the white flag. The high ground was lost, but Miles did not panic. The enemy's infantry could do little harm from Maryland and Loudoun Heights. Throughout the night of September 13, Miles concentrated on redeploying his force along the crest of his final stronghold—Bolivar Heights. He summoned Captain Charles H. Russell, 1st Maryland Cavalry, to deliver an urgent message. Miles knew Russell was familiar with the local roads and mountain paths, and he hoped he could squeeze through the Confederate stranglehold. Miles ordered Russell to "try to reach somebody that had ever heard of the United States Army, or any general of the United States Army, or anybody that knew anything about the United States Army, and report the condition of Harper's Ferry." Miles believed he could hold out for 48 hours—an occurrence not anticipated by Lee or Jackson in the execution of Special Orders 191.

Stonewall Jackson faced a serious dilemma on the night of September 13–14. Although pleased with the success of McLaws on Maryland Heights and Walker on Loudoun Heights, Miles still held an advantage—Bolivar Heights.

From his position on School House Ridge, 1,000 yards west of Bolivar Heights, Stonewall studied his opponent. The disadvantages for the Confederates became apparent. Bolivar Heights towered 200 feet above School House Ridge, providing the Federals with the high ground. Miles

Major General John G. Walker seized Loudoun Heights.(HFNHP)

Major General Lafayette McLaws battled for Maryland Heights. (LOC/PPOC)

Jackson's line extended nearly two miles along the crest of School House Ridge, stretching from the Potomac to the Shenandoah. Here appears the south portion of the ridge, as seen today. (NPS, PHOTOGRAPHER STEVE LOWE)

had positioned the bulk of his 14,000 men on Bolivar Heights, yielding numbers nearly equal to Jackson's force on School House Ridge. Most of the Union cannon were deployed atop Bolivar Heights, where they could sweep more than a half-mile of open ground. The rivers formed the flanks of Bolivar Heights, making it difficult to turn the position. Even if the Confederates utilized the river approaches, the vertical bluffs of Bolivar Heights made access problematic. Finally, Miles had an interior line that permitted rapid communication and potential for shifting troops to pressure points.

"The position before me is a strong one," Jackson admitted in a message to McLaws and Walker. Jackson never faced a stronger bulwark held by so many of the enemy.

An artillery bombardment developed as Jackson's first solution. However, moving his cannon to the crests presented a serious problem. Maryland Heights stretched 1,200 feet above the Potomac Valley. Loudoun Heights soared 900 feet above the Shenandoah shoreline. Hauling half-ton guns up these rugged slopes would be difficult, if not impossible. And, although he did not know it, Jackson was running short on time.

Near noon on September 13, about the time Jackson was aligning forces on School House Ridge, Union General McClellan was examining a communiqué found on the outskirts of Frederick. *It was a lost copy of Special Orders 191.* A jubilant McClellan telegrammed the President: "I think Lee has made a gross mistake."

> **"I have all the plans of the rebels and will catch them in their own trap. . . . Will send you trophies."**
>
> —**General George McClellan**

Jackson's position on School House Ridge, looking toward Bolivar Heights, as it appears today. In 1862, Bolivar Heights had been stripped of trees, so the Union defenders had a clear line of fire toward the Confederate lines. A frontal assault by Jackson was dubious, as his men would have to cross 1,000 yards of open fields and then scale a 300-foot vertical bluff to reach the Federal position. (NPS, Photographer Steve Lowe)

Bombardment

As McClellan plotted to strike Lee's divided and scattered army—including a rescue mission to Harpers Ferry—Jackson prodded his subordinates to hustle artillery to the crests of Maryland and Loudoun Heights. "Establish batteries wherever you can to take advantage, for the purpose of firing upon the enemy's camps, and at such other points as you may be able to damage him. . . . I desire to remain quiet, and let you . . . draw attention from [Bolivar Heights], so that I may have an opportunity of getting possession of the hill without much loss."

Sunday, September 14 was no day of rest for the hundreds of Confederates dragging cannon to the mountain crests. Fortunately, abandoned charcoal-haulers' roads on both Maryland and Loudoun Heights speeded the labor; and by 10:00 a.m., Walker had five rifled pieces on the Loudoun crest. Jackson welcomed the good news, but ordered Walker to wait. "I do not desire any of the batteries to open until all are ready on both sides of the river. . . . I will let you know when to open all the batteries."

Jackson showed some compassion on the Sabbath. "So soon as you get your batteries planted, let me know, as I desire . . . to send in a flag of truce, for the purpose of getting out the noncombatants, should the commanding officer refuse to surrender." At no other battlefield had Jackson had two residential towns in the sites of his cannon. Shells designed for soldiers could harm, or even kill, innocent people. Miles had not ensconced his men in houses or on the village streets, but in case the two towns became part of the battlefield, Jackson wanted citizens delivered from the danger—to a point. Stonewall's compassion was secondary

View of the southwestern end of Bolivar Heights from the Chambers (Murphy) Farm overlooking the Shenandoah River. (NPS, PHOTOGRAPHER STEVE LOWE)

to his military pragmatism. "Should we have to attack let the work be done thoroughly; fire on the houses when necessary. The citizens can keep out of harm's way from your artillery. Demolish the place if it is occupied by the enemy, and does not surrender."

"There was no corner of safety for unarmed men, women, and children," wrote Mary Clemmer Ames. "They could do nothing but look up to the frowning mountain walls and wait the storm of fire." From her perch on Camp Hill near the base hospital, the morning whistled with activity. Soldiers scurried to a nearby spring with their black coffee kettles, eager to stock their supply of water. Refugees from the Valley paced up and down

the streets, discussing the "probabilities of the day with troubled faces." Young girls and matrons passed to the hospital at the former paymaster's house that ominously overlooked the town graveyard. Hundreds of "contrabands" stood talking "in incoherent terror of 'Jackson' and the certainty of their 'being cotched and sold down South.'"

Trouble soon found Jackson. General Walker learned, in a signal message, that the Union army was threatening McLaws' rear. Walker relayed the concern to Jackson. Now aware of the unexpected Union thrust, Jackson stubbornly clung to his coordinated ring of fire. "Do not open until General McLaws notifies me what he can probably affect," he cautioned Walker. "Old Jack," a cannoneer in the Mexican War and the former instructor of artillery at the Virginia Military Institute, desired a textbook operation.

Modern interpretation of cannon poised to defend the Union position on Bolivar Heights. (NPS)

But Walker grew impatient. Concerned about his own division's vulnerability, Walker opened on his own. He ordered his five cannon to commence firing shortly after 1:00 p.m. "I saw two, three, four, half a dozen puffs of smoke burst out," recalled Captain Edward Hastings Ripley of the 9th Vermont Infantry from his post on Bolivar Heights. Suddenly, in the very center of the Union lines, "there was a crash, then another and another, and columns of dirt and smoke leaped into the air, as though a dozen young volcanoes had burst forth."

Within minutes, Jackson's artillerymen on School House Ridge were yanking lanyards, and by 2:00 p.m., four rifled pieces atop Maryland Heights were hurling shells from the north.

Colonel Miles' aide-de-camp, Lieutenant Henry Binney, was rattled by the intensity of the iron storm cascading from the mountaintops. "The cannonade is now terrific. The enemy's shell and shot fall in every direction; houses are demolished and detonation among the hills terrible." Mary Clemmer Ames scampered to her Camp Hill cellar and entrenched herself in an empty piano box "to escape the earthquake from above."

"They peppered us," proclaimed hospital Matron Abba Goddard from her stoop upon Camp Hill. "Some of our hospital tents were riddled by shell, but fortunately not one exploded." Goddard calmly beheld the cannonading. "After the first fire, one feels quite composed." No less than four unexploded shells and a slug fell within ten feet of the undaunted Matron. "As fast as a shell fell, I picked it up. The boys laughed to see me go and pick up my shells. . . . The slug, a piece of iron six inches long, being so hot I could not hold it. I held on to my trophies, however, and would have volunteered gathering the entire crop, had I supposed our gunners would have re-mailed them to Loudoun Heights."

"At first their missiles of death fell far short of our camp; but each succeeding shell came nearer and nearer, until the earth was plowed up at our feet, and our tents torn to tatters."

—Lieutenant James H. Clark, 115th New York Infantry

For the next five hours, more than 50 Confederate cannon mercilessly pounded Harpers Ferry. "A magnificent pyrotechnic display," admired one Rebel onlooker. The Federal gunners tried desperately to respond; but the Southerners' superior elevation and concentrated shell-fire rendered the

---

"The windows rattled; the house shook to its foundations. . . . Heaven and earth seemed collapsing."

—Mary Clemmer Ames

---

exposed Union artillery virtually useless. Walker's guns upon Loudoun Heights created the greatest consternation among the Union batteries. Just two hours after the bombardment commenced, Walker reported that he had "silenced" the Union battery on Camp Hill, using the former armory super-intendent's quarters as a rich target. The Federals admitted losing two guns and two caissons to the brisk fire and close range of the Rebel artillery atop Loudoun Heights.

"I am afraid of bombshells," Mary Clemmer Ames admitted. "If there is a sound purely devilish . . . it is the scream and shriek of a bombshell. No matter how thickly they tear the air, each fiend of a shell persists in a diaboli-cal individuality of its own, and never hisses or screams precisely like any one of its myriad neighbors."

Although the Confederate cannoneers found their Camp Hill targets, they caused little harm to the garrison's 11,000 infantrymen. Long and nar-row ravines cutting diagonally across Bolivar Heights granted limited cover and security to the human targets; but squeezing troops into a ravine consid-erably deflated the morale of the huddled blue masses.

"I tell you it is dreadful to be a mark for artillery," declared Captain Samuel Chapman Armstrong of the 125th New York. "Bad enough for any but especially for raw troops; it demoralizes them—it rouses one's courage to be able to fight in return, but to sit still and calmly be cut in two is too much to ask."

Despite the iron pouring down from the Southern artillery, Miles refused to yield. At dusk, the Stars and Stripes continued to float over Bolivar Heights.

Further complicating matters for Stonewall Jackson, a Union rescue column had approached to within six miles of Harpers Ferry. General McClellan, after his fortunate discovery of Lee's plans on September 13, had ordered Major General William B. Franklin to push the 12,000 men in his Sixth Corps to open a relief valve by approaching Maryland Heights from the north. "Your duty will be to cut off, destroy, or capture McLaws' command," McClellan stressed, "and relieve Colonel Miles." The follow-ing afternoon, a surprised McLaws maneuvered to protect his rear, delaying Franklin at Crampton's Gap in South Mountain long enough for nightfall

"A general feeling of depression observable in all the men. . . . All seem to think that we will have to surrender or be cut to pieces."

—Private Louis B. Hull,
60th Ohio

To
Shepherdstown

To
Sharpsburg

N
W E
S

0   500   1000
Yards

WARREN
JOHNSON

J.R. JONES
STARKE GRIGSBY

ARMISTEAD
FEATHERSTON
BARKSDALE
C.S. Signal Tower
KERSHAW

JACKSON

Naval Battery
Abandoned
Sept 13.

McLAWS

DUTASSY

MILES

WARD

LAWTON
EARLY
HAYS
WALKER
DOUGLAS

FORD

TRIMBLE

MANNING

C.S. Signal Tower

WALKER

To
Charlestown

PENDER
THOMAS

RANSOM

A.P. HILL
BROCKENBROUGH
ARCHER
BRANCH
GREGG

(MAP BY GENE THORP © 2000)

90

to stall the Union advance. But McLaws' situation was desperate. His force of 8,000 was trapped in Pleasant Valley, just north of the Ferry. If the Rebel noose didn't strangle the defiant garrison, McLaws himself might become the unwitting victim.

Meanwhile, Colonel Miles had no idea that allies were so close. He had no view of Franklin at South Mountain and had received no communication indicating Franklin's mission or presence. Sunday afternoon's bombardment muffled any sound of Franklin's fight at Crampton's Gap. From Colonel Miles' perspective, he was surrounded, isolated, and with no help in sight. "Oh, where is McClellan and his army?" Miles puzzled. Echoing too were those resolute orders from headquarters: "You will not abandon Harper's Ferry without defending it to the last extremity."

The Cavalry Escape

At approximately 7:00 p.m. on Sunday, Benjamin Franklin "Grimes" Davis and his fellow cavalry commanders met with Colonel Miles at his headquarters. Davis, a West Point graduate and regular army veteran, spoke the same military language of Miles. No one else in the garrison of 14,000 had the army bona fides of Grimes Davis. Miles listened intently as Davis explained that the cavalry was of no use to the besieged garrison, but could be useful as a breakout force. If the cavalry could find a hole in the Confederate stranglehold, then perhaps it could escape and seek assistance.

The odds weren't good, but Miles deemed the scheme worth the risk. He ordered the cavalry to make "immediate preparations to leave here at 8:00 [p.m.] without baggage wagons, ambulances, or lead horses." The column must move swiftly and silently, without encumbrances. In addition, they must keep the movement a secret, for "if the infantry became aware of it, it would cause a stampede among them."

Following debate about the route of escape, Miles directed his 1,400 horsemen to cross the Potomac River pontoon bridge, then turn left, and head north via the Harpers Ferry–Sharpsburg Road. "No other instruction can be given to the commander," Miles concluded, "than to force his way through the enemy's line and join our army." One Rhode Island trooper predicted: "By morning, [we] would be in Pennsylvania, on the way to Richmond, or in Hell!" As darkness enveloped the town, a column of shadowy horsemen stretched along Shenandoah Street. Promptly at 8:00 p.m., the lead scouts reached the armory boat ramp and swaying pontoon bridge. One by one each nervous trooper silently crossed the river. They rode with uncertainty. There was not one shot or sound. Where were the Rebels? Were the Confederates sleeping or simply unaware of what was happening?

Union belt buckle. (Courtesy Photographer Lemeul B. Muniz, Assistant Photographer Johnathan G. Stopiak)

Hundreds of Confederates strained throughout the night to drag cannon up steep ravines on the Chambers Farm, working quietly to avoid enemy detection. (NPS/HFCCAC/Artist Hugh Brown)

Fortuitously for the Union riders, just hours before the escape commenced, Confederate General McLaws had opened the door of opportunity by withdrawing most of the Southerners holding Maryland Heights, redeploying them north into Pleasant Valley to counter the Union threat at Crampton's Gap. By dawn, not only had the entire column escaped, it also had seized a Confederate munitions train near Williamsport and escorted it north into Pennsylvania. Unfortunately for Colonel Miles, he knew nothing of these successes. For as his cavalry was escaping, Stonewall began to stir.

General Jackson had lost patience. Disappointed his cannon had not brought submission, and frustrated by the stubborn and unexpected resistance of the Federals, Jackson knew his slow progress now threatened the entire Confederate army. Stonewall also accepted that artillery alone would not reduce the enemy. He must attack.

Based upon his intimate knowledge of the terrain, his plan called for three maneuvers: a flanking march and attack against the enemy's left on Bolivar Heights; a feigned assault against the Union right center as a diversion; and a flanking march and redeployment of 10 cannon to the base of Loudoun Heights.

Each maneuver occurred in the darkness of September 14–15. As the Stonewall Division launched a night demonstration toward the Federal right and center—forcing Miles to pull troops away from his left—A. P. Hill's division skirted the Shenandoah and slipped into positions behind the Union left on the Chambers Farm and along the southern end of Bolivar Heights (ironically, held, only hours before, by the escaping cavalry). Meanwhile, in a remarkable artillery flanking march, 10 guns moved from School House Ridge, across the Shenandoah, then scaled Loudoun Heights to a shelf overlooking (and from where cannon could enfilade) the Bolivar Heights ravines.

Major General Ambrose Powell Hill conducted the nighttime flanking maneuver that forced the Union surrender. When Hill seized the southwestern end of Bolivar Heights along the Shenandoah River, he pronounced, "The fate of Harper's Ferry is sealed." (HFNHP)

"The infernal screech owls came hissing and singing, then bursting, plowing great holes in the earth, filling our eyes with dust, and tearing many giant trees to atoms."

—James H. Clark, 115th New York

At dawn on Monday, September 15, a thick fog blanketed the Harpers Ferry garrison, concealing both armies' positions. When a brisk, raw wind funneled through the water gap, the fog lifted above the hills. Then, the cannon erupted.

Surrender

Confederate battery in position at the Chambers (Murphy) Farm today. Cannon like this fired into the Union left flank and rear at less than 800 yards—point blank range for Civil War artillery— making it impossible for Federal infantry to form and fight. (NPS, Photographer Steve Lowe)

"We are surrounded by [the] enemy's batteries," recalled Lieutenant Binney. "Nothing could stand before such a raking cannonade." Captain Edward Ripley of the 9th Vermont concurred: "We are as hapless as rats in a cage."

The situation had changed dramatically for Dixon Miles. During 11 hours of darkness, Jackson had deployed 5,000 infantrymen and 20 cannon on his left flank at close range, and positioned artillery at point-blank range on a high plateau upon Loudoun Heights to fire into the previously secure Bolivar Heights ravines. Just before 8:00 a.m., Miles' battery commanders reported their long-range ammunition exhausted. Without artillery to support his infantry, Miles believed further resistance now useless.

Following a council of war, Miles and his commanders unanimously agreed to surrender.

Miles immediately began spreading the word, traveling along the crest of Bolivar Heights with white handkerchiefs in the air. He exhorted his men to raise the white flag. "Boys, we've got no country now," cried Eugene McGrath of the 5th New York Heavy Artillery. Louis Hull's diary reflected similar anguish: "15th Monday a rather dark page [in] the history of us."

As white flags began bobbing along the crest of Bolivar Heights, the hopeful Confederates ceased firing—but only momentarily. Apparently

uncertain of the Federal intentions or unaware of the displayed white flags, a Southern battery on the Niswarner Farm on a plateau near the base of Loudoun Heights launched its shells once again toward the Union left.

"The rebels have opened on us again," Miles declared. "What do they mean?"

Immediately after this query, a shell whizzed past Miles and his aide, Lieutenant Binney. It exploded directly behind the two officers, and a large piece of iron ripped the flesh entirely from Colonel Miles' left calf. The next day, Miles reportedly said that he "had done his duty" and was "an old soldier and willing to die." The man who surrendered Harpers Ferry died at his headquarters at the master armorer's house, leaving behind many unanswered questions.

Private Louis B. Hull was one of the thousands of Federal soldiers pinned down by the Confederate bombardment. (HFNHP)

Colonel Miles raced on horseback from battery to battery, ordering his artillerymen to cease firing following the decision to surrender. (HFNHP)

"Through God's blessing," Jackson scribbled in a note to General Lee, "Harper's Ferry and its garrison are to be surrendered." Lee received the message about noon on September 15 at his position near Antietam Creek. Here, he made his decision to stand in Maryland and reunite the army near Sharpsburg. Two days later, both armies would endure the bloodiest day in American history.

Posthumous Blame

Embarrassed by the Harpers Ferry surrender, the United States government, the military, and the press all demanded answers. Everyone knew something had gone wrong. Subsequently, eight days following the capitulation of September 15, 1862, the War Department ordered a special

Colonel Miles poses at Harpers Ferry one month before his surrender and death. (LOC)

commission to investigate the surrender of Harpers Ferry. Major General David Hunter, a friend of the Lincoln administration and the man who later led the tribunal which tried the Lincoln assassination conspirators, presided over the proceedings. Since Colonel Dixon Miles could not defend himself, his son, a physician, represented him.

Piecing together the Harpers Ferry puzzle took 15 days of testimony from 44 witnesses, ranging in rank from lieutenant to major general and included several civilians. Questions ranged from: "From what you know of Colonel Miles as a military man, do you think he was morally, mentally, and physically competent to command?" to queries about accusations of drunkenness and even treason. The testimony produced over 900 pages of evidence.

"An officer who cannot appear before any earthly tribunal," opined the court after only two days of deliberation, "is entitled to the tenderest care and most careful investigation." The commission cleared Colonel Miles of intoxication or treason, yet unabashedly declared that Miles' "incapacity, amounting to almost imbecility, led to the shameful surrender of this important post." Even today, Dixon Miles' reputation suffers from this permanent branding of incompetence.

An Ungodly Crew

*T*he Confederate victory reaped 73 captured cannon, 200 wagons, 1,200 army mules, about 13,000 small arms, and nearly 12,700 Union prisoners— the largest surrender of United States troops during the Civil War. No other Confederate victory matched these materiel results.

Silence replaced the thunder of cannon as Union Brigadier General Julius White rode to meet Stonewall Jackson to negotiate the details of the surrender. Crossing Bolivar Heights in the direction of School House Ridge, White first encountered Henry Kyd Douglas (Jackson's youngest staff officer) and then General A. P. Hill. Following introductions, the two Confederates escorted the Union brigadier to Jackson. "There was nothing strikingly military" about General White's appearance, Kyd Douglas recorded. But striking indeed was the contrast between White and Jackson. "White was mounted on a handsome black horse, was handsomely uniformed, with an untarnished sabre, immaculate gloves and boots, and had a staff fittingly equipped. . . . He must have been somewhat astonished to find in General Jackson the worst-dressed, worst mounted, most faded and dingy-looking general he had ever seen anyone surrender to."

The interview between the two generals was brief. White asked for terms. Jackson called for unconditional surrender. When White formally capitulated Jackson ordered A. P. Hill to work out the details. With that, the discussion ended. "We expected to be stripped of everything," wrote the 126th New York's Nicholas DeBraff as he buried his revolver and marked the spot. But General Hill granted quite liberal terms to his captives. All U.S. property of "every description" would be surrendered. Officers, however, would be allowed to retain their private property and sidearms.

Brigadier General Julius White (LOC)

Jackson reviews the defeated Federals. (NPS/HFCCAC/Hugh Brown)

As General Jackson trotted toward Harpers Ferry to examine the fruits of his victory, he became the featured attraction for thousands of Federals. "Boys, he's not much for looks," shouted one Northerner, "but if we'd had him we wouldn't have been caught in this trap." Jackson's drab appearance disappointed many within the Union ranks. "Old Stonewall dressed in the coarsest of homespun, and dirty at that," witnessed *New York Times* correspondent David Judd. In appearance, the reporter continued, Jackson could not be distinguished from "the mongrel, barefoot crew who follow his fortunes. I had heard much of the decayed appearance of the rebel soldiers; but such a looking crowd! Ireland, in her worst straits, could present no parallel."

One Union soldier in the 126th New York noticed that the fresh Confederate victory could not disguise "the poverty of their clothing and equipments, their sallow, hungry faces, their long, tangled hair and slouched hats, and their gaunt frames which seemed nothing but bone and muscle covered with a bronzed skin." As Louis B. Hull eyed his opponents, he declared them "the dirtiest and greasiest set I ever saw."

Hospital Matron Goddard wrote of the Rebel appearance: "God forbid my ever looking upon such an ungodly crew again. . . . Just suppose a meal bag draggled through the mud, dipped in bacon fat, and stuffed with rags, animated, and you have a decent representation of a live secesh—especially the live part—for the vermin frequently dropped from their clothes as they walked the street."

In striking contrast to the Confederates stood the well-equipped, recently uniformed, immaculately manicured Federals. "These troops had not been in active service," observed Confederate cavalryman W. W. Blackford, "and in their luxurious garrison life they looked as if they had come out of [a] bandbox, with their untarnished uniforms, white shirt collars, and polished boots."

Insignia of the 32nd Ohio Infantry. (HFNHP, NPS, Photographer Marsha Wassel)

The formal surrender stirred both Northern and Southern emotions. *Richmond Examiner* editor Edward Pollard best described the Southern perspective: "The scene of the surrender was one of deep humiliation to the North," he began. "It was indeed a repetition of the revolutionary glories of Yorktown, to see here the proud, gayly dressed soldiers of the oppressor drawn up in line, stacking their arms, and surrendering to the ragged, barefoot, half-starved soldiers of liberty." Sergeant Charles E. Smith of the 32nd Ohio Infantry witnessed the event with impassioned outrage: "They hoisted the bars and stars where one hour before our glorious old star-spangled banner floated proudly in the breeze. Oh, how my heart beat and my bosom heaved to see that corrupt flag raised in defiance over us."

Despite her disdain for the Confederate cause, Matron Goddard did admire the Confederate conviction. After conversing with a few of the conquerors she wrote: "As a body, the army is weary of the war—but they say they are in for the war . . . I asked several if they had ever been paid. They said no, not a cent. We don't fight for pay—we fight for victory."

Soon after the surrender ceremony concluded, thousands of hungry Confederates began rummaging through their captured booty. "We fared sumptuously," declared J. F. J. Caldwell of Maxy Gregg's South Carolina brigade. "In addition to meat, crackers, sugar, coffee, shoes, blankets, underclothing, etc., many of us captured horses roaming at large, on whom to transport our plunder."

"The rage, the indignation, the surprise, the mortification of [12,000] men, and one woman, it is impossible for me to describe."
—**Matron Abba A. Goddard**

The Southern veterans had just a short time to frolic and rest. Robert E. Lee was in trouble. The Union army attacked the gaps of South Mountain, forcing the Confederates to retreat to the Antietam Creek. Here Lee stood without two-thirds of his army, the Potomac River separating the commands. Lee ordered Stonewall to hurry north to assist him in an expected face off with the Federals. "Ah, this is all very well," Jackson informed a Confederate major when reflecting upon his Harpers Ferry success, "but we have yet much hard work before us." Promptly at 12:01 a.m. on September 16, Jackson's men started for Sharpsburg, Maryland.

Jackson's Confederates suffered few casualties in their Harpers Ferry triumph. Two days later, many of Stonewall's men, like those of Longstreet's Corps seen in this photo, were killed or wounded during the Battle of Antietam in the bloodiest day in American history. (LOC)

Parole

As Jackson's "foot cavalry" raced away, the surrendered bluecoats commenced their own march in an opposite direction. General A. P. Hill's force was left behind at the Ferry to deal with the 12,700 prisoners of war. Hill promptly "paroled" the Union prisoners. In a unique agreement negotiated between North and South in August 1862, a released or "paroled" prisoner of war could not conduct any aspect of warfare until he was "exchanged" for an enemy POW. A paroled prisoner could not fight, cook, drive mules, serve as a medic or nurse, build forts, or do anything associated with the war. Once exchanged, the parole ended, and the soldier could return to active duty. Each side promised to abide by the provisions of the parole agreement, gentleman's honor being the sole enforcer.

By the terms of surrender, all Federals captured at Harpers Ferry would return north with the promise not to serve against the Confederacy until exchanged for an equal number of Confederate parolees. General Hill did not have time to parole thousands of individuals, so he devised a system of mass parole. The conquered Yankees mustered in company formations, heard the roll called, listened to the parole statement, raised their right hands, and then promised in unison not to fight until exchanged. Company and/or regimental officers signed for their commands, and individual officers then signed their own parole statement.

"It makes us feel ashamed marching before the enemy without guns," lamented Louis B. Hull of the 60th Ohio Infantry. Many, however, disabled their guns, removing the spring from the lock (thus rendering them useless) prior to stacking them for the enemy's collection. "Cartloads of broken muskets lie about in every encampment," observed hospital Matron Goddard. Some shielded their flags from the Rebel captors. One brigade officer ordered his regimental flag bearers to stash the Stars and Stripes into his private baggage. The color bearer of the 32nd Ohio Infantry wrapped his regimental flag around his body under his clothes. The 115th New York stripped its staffs and replaced the colors with oil cloth wrapped tightly in canvas. The 125th New York shredded its flag and distributed the pieces throughout the regiment. With or without colors, Federal regiments began stomping across the pontoon bridge into Maryland during the late morning of September 16.

No Confederates accompanied the Federal parolees as they marched toward Frederick, Maryland. The opportunity to violate parole was great. Just north of the Ferry was a large contingent of the main Union army—a tempting

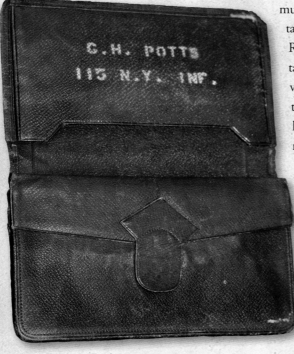

Wallet of Private C. H. Potts whose unit surrendered at Harpers Ferry on September 15, 1862. (HFNHP, Jeff Bowers Collection, NPS, Photographer Marsha Wassel)

"I'll sell my life for these free boys."

As the surrendered 60th Ohio Regiment awaited its turn to cross the Potomac River, Colonel William Trimble stopped at General A. P. Hill's headquarters to obtain passes for 13 free blacks that had accompanied the regiment from Ohio. Trimble had previously negotiated with Hill on their safe passage, and though Hill was reluctant because he could not determine between slaves and freemen, he agreed to trust Colonel Trimble. Thus, with passes in hand, Trimble rode to the river.

Here he discovered trouble. Trimble's regiment had been halted and refused passage onto the pontoon bridge. A Rebel guard stood with crossed bayonets. Even more disconcerting were the Confederates moving through Trimble's ranks and "dragging the colored boys from their positions near the officers." Trimble demanded the meaning of this inquisition. The response—he was a thief, stealing their slaves, and that the command wouldn't pass until "every slave was taken out." Trimble explained that his men were free blacks, and that he had passes from General Hill. The Confederate officer in charge refused to acknowledge or accept Hill's authority in this case. Trimble had enough. "My men are unarmed—I am not!" he shouted. "I'll sell my life for these free boys. Unhand them! Guards, give way! Regiment, march!" The Confederates stepped aside, and the free blacks marched across the pontoon with the 60th Ohio. These men "felt like a new birth of freedom had been vouchsafed them."

Colonel William Trimble
(Nicholas Picerno Collection)

---

sanctuary of refuge. Yet not a single Northern parolee yielded to this temptation. Instead, they arrived at Annapolis on September 21 as a "sorry lot of men and homesick as a lot of dogs with nothing to eat."

Four months later, all Harpers Ferry parolees were declared exchanged and returned to the ranks. Ironically, at the Battle of Gettysburg in July 1863, many of the former Harpers Ferry prisoners faced their former captors, stopping a Confederate attack on the second day of the battle, and saving the Union position on Cemetery Ridge. The victory at Gettysburg finally wiped away the ignominious stain of surrender.

As the paroled prisoners marched out of Harpers Ferry on September 16, General A. P. Hill, instructed to transport everything to Winchester, busily tended to the removal of the captured goods. Hill knew he had little time, as the prospect for battle loomed in nearby Maryland. Throughout the day Hill's men loaded captured U.S. wagons with commissary supplies: 155,954 pounds of hard bread, 19,267 pounds of bacon, 1,545 pounds of salt-beef, 1,315 pounds of salt-pork, and 4,903 pounds of coffee. Teamsters hitched up hundreds of U.S. branded mules which hauled thousands of small arms and ammunition boxes to Winchester. Dozens of cannon and caissons rumbled up the Valley to Lee's staging area. As Jackson's chief quartermaster noted: "Many worn-out wagons were exchanged for good Yankee ones, the useless ones being left behind."

One outcome of the Confederate capture received little notoriety. General Hill also confiscated former slaves who recently had fled to Harpers Ferry. Declaring any escaped slave legal property, Hill methodically rounded up the African Americans who had ventured to the Ferry and sought shelter behind the Union lines. "Every nook, corner, cranny, barn, and stye has been searched," wrote Matron Goddard, "and men, women, and little children in droves, have been carried off . . . our hospital laundresses, and our men servants, without a word of warning, were seized upon and carried [away]." Although official Confederate records enumerated everything from number of horseshoes captured to pounds of sugar, no Confederate record identified the number of former slaves seized at Harpers Ferry. Some unofficial accounts claimed as many as 2,000 blacks were escorted south and returned to slavery.

Mrs. Goddard refused to allow seven of her most intimate black companions to be taken. "I am almost tired of night-watching, and my revolver begins to grow heavy. It holds but five balls, but before secesh gets my seven ebonies, my body will pay for the two balls wanting. Oh, this traffic in human flesh!"

Shortly after dawn on September 17, A. P. Hill received urgent orders to rush to Sharpsburg. The Battle of Antietam had commenced, and the outnumbered Lee needed every available Confederate in his army. Since Hill had not completed the removal of captured supplies, he left behind one brigade of about 1,000 men to finish the operation. About 7:30 a.m. he raced north. Eight hours later, Hill's weary men smashed into Major General Ambrose Burnside, leading the third Union assault of the day across the Antietam Creek. Hill's timely arrival stopped the Federal advance and the battle ended.

Early the next evening explosions rocked the water gap at Harpers Ferry. Large fires broke out, burning the pontoon bridge and the government storehouses in the old armory buildings. "All the property the Rebels could not move

from Harper's Ferry they have destroyed," reported a Union scout. Matron Goddard recalled the scene: "They finished up by burning carload after carload of rice and beans; the air even now is full of the odor of burning beans."

The iron spans of the bridge were "blown up and laying in confused masses in the river." Spans crossing the armory waste weirs and the armory canal were in ruins. The railroad's carpenter shop, tool house, and blacksmith shop were gutted. Ten boxcars were torched and three gondola cars run into the river. The waste of four more boxcars and two crane cars lay in the C&O Canal. B&O Engine No. 30 was burned and "hanging in trestlework at west end of the bridge," and Engine No. 166 was a charred iron bucket resting just upstream from the armory. The bridge piers remained undamaged, standing as stone sentinels despite five Rebel attempts to blow them up. Two weeks later, B&O work crews had the railroad bridge reopened for the fourth time in 15 months.

Remains of the Musket Factory, as viewed from Potomac Street, showing the remnants of the former armory and the destroyed Union supply base. (NARA)

Following Jackson's capture of Harpers Ferry, the Confederates torched the U.S. Armory Depot buildings, toppled sections of the railroad bridge, and pulled the planks from the pontoon bridge. This image, taken by photographer Matthew Brady, appeared in Harper's Weekly *as a pen and ink sketch October 4, 1862.* (LOC)

Reoccupation

*W*hen the Confederates retreated into the Shenandoah Valley following the Battle of Antietam, the Union army hurriedly reoccupied Harpers Ferry. The first Federals appeared on Maryland Heights on September 19, where they encountered a horrible odor. "Many bodies were still unburied," recalled Major General Alpheus Williams, as he witnessed local people scouring the recent Maryland Heights battlefield, picking up abandoned firearms. Remains, both Union and Confederate, lay scattered across the mountaintop. Citizens from nearby Sandy Hook attempted burial, but the almost soilless stone ridge made the task nearly impossible.

"All about us was the wreckage of September 13th and the unburied bodies of both armies," wrote Miles Huyett of the 125th Pennsylvania Infantry. "To minimize the danger of pestilence the only thing we could do was to gather brush and logs and burn the bodies of the dead." J. Strait, a Union soldier in an unidentified New York regiment, confirmed Huyett's account. "They had just got the rebels burnt . . . we saw the bones of them." Most of the remains were Confederate, and some attempt was made to throw dirt over the burned bodies. "The graves had been made so shallow," described Private Rice C. Bull of the recently organized 123rd New York Infantry, "that many of the bodies were partly uncovered by the rain, so that hands and feet and even heads were visible. This was a gruesome sight for new soldiers."

The sight of Union soldiers on Maryland Heights was glorious to hospital Matron Goddard. "Our bluecoats are just coming [into view], and I have screamed myself hoarse in gladness. . . . Who they are, or where from, we cannot as yet tell, but they are blue coats and carry muskets. We can see the bayonets glitter in the sun."

Shortly after the Federal reoccupation of Maryland Heights, men from the Union signal service arrived on the high peak, "wav[ing] their flags in the clear air, announcing that the stars and stripes again floated over the whole of Maryland." Signal flags were a principal form of communication for the Union army. From Showman's Knoll

*This Union signal station atop Loudoun Heights used flag motions to communicate messages to Maryland Heights (background) and other surrounding stations. With the mountainous terrain about Harpers Ferry, flag signals proved more expeditious and economical in transmitting observations or orders than telegraph wires or couriers. (*Harper's Weekly;* Flag courtesy NPS, HFC)*

near General McClellan's headquarters south of Sharpsburg, orders and observations could be transmitted direct to the Maryland Heights station. From there the flagmen would signal to Sugar Loaf Mountain, located about midway between Maryland Heights and Washington. And from Sugar Loaf, a message could be received at the capital. This system of sending coded messages via flag waving proved very effective and was timelier than horse-riding couriers and more economical and secure than stringing telegraph wires.

Among the first to occupy Maryland Heights was the 2nd Massachusetts Infantry. "The place did not look natural," remembered Chaplain Alonzo Quint,

upon his return to the campground his regiment had occupied 13 months before. "The land had been stripped of its trees; and the old paths to the spring, and down to the river, were bald and shelterless." The war not only had ravaged the land, but the regiment. Dozens in the "Harvard Regiment" had died or been wounded in battle during the 1862 campaigns; dozens more had succumbed to disease. The regimental flag symbolized their ordeal at Antietam—20 new bullet holes through the colors and three cavities through the staff. After seven months of hard campaigning, the survivors relaxed. "I think at last we are going to have a little rest," wrote Charles Morse, as he watched a sunset from Maryland Heights.

The first U.S. troops to reenter Harpers Ferry following the Confederate departure occurred in the darkness of September 19. An infantry detachment

After the Confederate's first invasion of the North ended in retreat, nearly 60,000 Union soldiers encamped in or around Harpers Ferry. To help prevent another incursion, General McClellan intended to make the Ferry a "permanent and secure occupation." (DENNIS E. FRYE COLLECTION, SKETCH BY A. LUMLEY)

General John W. Geary's Union division crosses the Shenandoah pontoon bridge and begins its ascent up Loudoun Heights during the Federal reoccupation of Harpers Ferry. The piers in the background are remnants of the bridge destroyed by the Confederates during the war's first summer. (FRANK LESLIE'S ILLUSTRATED NEWSPAPER)

discovered a ford two feet deep, then carefully waded the slippery Potomac. They found no enemy, but did discover 300 wounded and sick Union soldiers at the base hospital at the former paymaster's quarters on Camp Hill. They also found a fresh graveyard on the grounds of the hospital. Matron Goddard reported, "We have buried seventeen men just opposite my window, under an apple tree, without shroud or coffin."

Three days later the Federals began fording the river in force. "This was rather unpleasant," complained a wet Joseph Ward of the 106th Pennsylvania Infantry. "It was an animating scene," contended Charles D. Page of the 14th Connecticut Infantry. "The band leading the way, playing *Jordan is a Hard Road to Travel, Way Down South in Dixie, Yankee Doodle,* and *Old Virginia.*" Page was also humored by the literal missteps of his comrades. "Every now and then some unfortunate weight would be carried off his feet . . . and would go under the water, blowing like a porpoise."

Only five days after his regiment's indoctrination at Antietam's Bloody Lane, Page considered it "merry work crossing the stream. . . . There was a feeling of exhilaration as [we] passed by the ruins of the arsenal where John Brown had fought so stoutly, the band playing *Glory Hallelujah.*" It was September 22, the same day Abraham Lincoln had decreed a new direction for the war. The President had just announced his *Preliminary Emancipation Proclamation.* With that, Lincoln changed the Northern purpose from a war not only to preserve the Union, but to ensure freedom for every American.

Lincoln's Visit

On September 23, the Federal army rapidly reestablished a foothold in Harpers Ferry with the arrival of new pontoons to replace the burned-out bridge. The fresh white canvas of the pontoons presented a stark contrast to "the most complete wreck of a city." John D. Smith of the 19th Maine Infantry wrote of "the shattered and decaying dwellings, prostrate forests, and ruined works of art." Smith concluded Harpers Ferry "is almost a bed of ashes." After spending some time among the crumbling walls of the old armory, he sagely predicted: "In future years traveler and tourist will eagerly resort [here] . . . and history will point out [this] as the spot where many acts in the great tragedy, not yet closed, took place."

George McClellan viewed Harpers Ferry from a different, more strategic, perspective. When he ascended Maryland Heights on September 26, McClellan spied his nemesis spread across the lower Shenandoah Valley. Here, he deemed the occupation of Harpers Ferry "a military necessity." Seeing the once-again destroyed railroad bridge, he conceived "it is necessary to build a permanent double-track bridge over the Potomac . . . [and] also a wagon bridge over the Shenandoah." The heights had to be fortified "in order to avoid a similar catastrophe to the one which happened to Colonel Miles." Until the double-track railroad bridge was completed, "it is scarcely possible to advance from Harper's Ferry, in force, as that is clearly our true line of operations." Any delay in an advance against the enemy—and McClellan had a reputation for procrastination—set off alarms in Washington. "I know the Government does not contemplate the delay in your movements for the length of time required to build permanent bridges," wired General-in-Chief Henry W. Halleck.

This prospect of delay so concerned President Lincoln that he decided to pay a personal visit to McClellan. Lincoln desired to prod his general into striking the recently retreated Rebels, now nearby in the Valley, using the good fall weather to McClellan's advantage. Lincoln also wished to personally appear before the soldiers of the Army of the Potomac and thank them for defeating the Confederate invasion.

Traveling via the B&O Railroad, the chief executive and his presidential party arrived at Harpers Ferry about noon on October 1. Since the bridge had not yet been repaired, Lincoln walked into the Confederacy via the new pontoon bridge. Passing up the armory boat ramp, the first building the president witnessed was the John Brown Fort. The president was escorted to Bolivar Heights—"the summit and sides of which

> *"I never knew that a town could be so willfully desolated by the hands of men . . . it looks awful."*
>
> **—William Reichard, 128th Pennsylvania Infantry**

President Abraham Lincoln. (*The Soldier in Our Civil War*, 1885, Frank Leslie)

swarm with infantry, artillery, cavalry, baggage trains, and all the appurtenances belonging to a campaign." This scene juxtaposed the beauty of the natural landscape. It "really seem[ed] too lovely to be the seat of a horrid war," mused Dunn Browne of the 18th Connecticut Infantry from his new camp on Bolivar Heights, "a paradise too sweet for the Devil to enter with his polluting presence. But the devil of war is a mighty fiend, and he is laying his strong hand of desolation heavily on this particular region."

Atop Bolivar Heights President Lincoln reviewed nearly 15,000 men of the Union 2nd Corps, where only two weeks before Stonewall Jackson had viewed nearly as many captured Federals. This was a happier occasion for the boys in blue, as the president acknowledged the veterans of Antietam's fierce engagements in the West Woods and at Bloody Lane. Joseph Ward of the 106th Pennsylvania related how the men of the 2nd Corps "manifested their pleasure with the visit, and their affection for that great and good man . . . by long and continued cheers and the president's salute of twenty-one guns."

Reviewing the men from horseback, Lincoln proved an interesting spectacle to the troops. "The great, noble man was a poor horseman, and awkwardly sat [on] his horse," wrote Edwin Bryant of the 3rd Wisconsin Infantry. "The men, at order arms, cheered with a will; and as a cloud of caps flew high in the air, the President's horse began to jump and caper." Bryant witnessed hundreds

President Lincoln reviewed Federal troops during his visit to Harpers Ferry. (NPS/HFCCAC/Hugh Brown)

of eyes watching as "the president swung his long legs under the horse, clapped one hand on the top of his high hat, and doubled up, presenting an appearance so ludicrous that a suppressed titter burst from the whole line."

President Lincoln spent the night in Harpers Ferry at the headquarters of the 2nd Corps commander, Major General Edwin Sumner. From Bolivar Heights, Lincoln witnessed an impressive night show. "The sight was a grand one as the great army encamped over these hills and the view at night of thousands of campfires illuminated the hills from base to summit," wrote Charles Page of the 14th Connecticut. In addition to the "innumerable camp fires glimmering in every direction," the President likely listened to "the jargon of bugles and drums which at stated times call out the army for roll-calls." As the army settled for the evening, a "hum of voices like that of an immense city . . . arose from the valleys on either side and filled the air with a confusion of sounds."

Mr. Lincoln rose early on October 2 for a full day of reviews, travel, and meetings with top commanders. He first rode across the Shenandoah and ascended Loudoun Heights to visit the division of John W. Geary. Geary, returning to the Harpers Ferry area for the third time in a year, clad himself in full-dress uniform and commenced the presidential review at precisely 8:00 a.m. "This was a quiet review," recalled William H. H. Tallman of the 66th Ohio Infantry. The narrow mountain shelf afforded "no room for maneuvering troops at this camp [so] we simply marched by and saluted." General Geary noticed how the war had affected the President: "Abraham looks quite care worn and not nearly so well as he did when I last saw him."

After Loudoun Heights the presidential party crossed over to Maryland Heights to review the Federal 12th Corps. "I had quite a long talk with [the President], sitting on a pile of logs," General Alpheus Williams informed his family. "He's really the most unaffected, simple-minded, honest, and frank man I have ever met. . . . I wish he had a little more firmness, though I suppose the main difficulty with him is to make up his mind as to the best policy amongst the multitude of advisers and advice." Following the formal review, Lieutenant Charles F. Morse of the 2nd Massachusetts Infantry received instructions to guide the presidential party to the summit of Maryland Heights. "I showed the way until we got to a path where it was right straight up, when Abraham backed out," related Morse. "I think it must have reminded him of a little story about a very steep place; at any rate, around they turned and went down the mountain."

By noon on October 2, Lincoln had completed his Harpers Ferry visit and started toward McClellan's headquarters south of Sharpsburg. For the next two days, he reviewed the remainder of the Army of the Potomac, visited landmarks on the fields of Antietam, and met repeatedly with General McClellan. The two leaders, who had a strained and distrusting relationship, agreed that a move against the enemy must occur. They did not concur, however, on where and when. Harpers Ferry became central in the debate between the President and his field commander over the direction of the war.

Lincoln and McClellan near Sharpsburg, Maryland, following Lincoln's visit to Harpers Ferry. (LOC)

General McClellan ordered Maryland Heights fortified to ensure no more Union disasters befell the Harpers Ferry garrisons. (Dennis E. Frye Collection)

McClellan's plans for Harpers Ferry included the permanent railroad bridge, the fortifications, and the establishment of a base of operations; and he pleaded with the President for time to complete his Harpers Ferry efforts before striking the Confederates. Lincoln remained unimpressed. Two days after departing Sharpsburg, the President instructed McClellan—in no uncertain terms—to advance against the Rebels. "The President directs that you cross the Potomac and give battle to the enemy or drive him south," General-in-Chief Halleck asserted in an October 6 dictate. "Your army must move now while the roads are good."

McClellan did not commence his advance until 20 days later. In the interim, the commander continued to focus upon fortifying Harpers Ferry. At McClellan's request, he received an ambitious fortification plan, surveyed and laid out by an enterprising engineer, Lieutenant Cyrus B. Comstock. Comstock proposed "a line of stone blockhouses or redoubts" stretching one and one half miles from the Potomac upon the crests of both Maryland and Loudoun Heights. This plan developed an "entrenched camp" suitable for 3,000 men at an estimated cost of $50,000. General-in-Chief Halleck responded: "This project of extensively fortifying Harper's Ferry, and constructing a permanent bridge at that point involves a very considerable expenditure of money, a larger garrison, and a long delay, perhaps extending into winter." McClellan countered with his own assessment. "I look upon the permanent and secure occupation of Harper's Ferry as a military necessity." Halleck pulled rank and funding. "Harper's Ferry is not, in my opinion, a proper base of operations . . . it would be an error to expend time and money there for such an object." The

Secretary of War terminated the argument on October 20, when he approved Halleck's proposal to make Washington the base of operations, reducing Harpers Ferry to "field defenses, with a moderate garrison."

While the argument festered between McClellan and the Lincoln administration, the general commenced construction of fortifications at the Ferry. A line of earthworks soon stretched across vulnerable Bolivar Heights. Opposite Bolivar Heights, on the Maryland side of the Potomac, a large rectangular work named "Fort Duncan" was shoveled and piled into place. Atop Maryland Heights, a battery of long-range artillery was established and entrenched; and at the Naval Battery, permanent earthen walls were excavated to replace the old sandbag defenses. Most impressive, at the highest point on the mountain, masons began chipping and carving massive rocks into a blockhouse christened the "Stone Fort." To assist with this back-breaking labor, McClellan requisitioned 2,000 contraband slaves from Washington—an intriguing request, considering the President had just issued his *Preliminary Emancipation Proclamation*. General Halleck initially endorsed this

This Maryland Heights fort hosted 30-pounder (the weight of the projectile) rifled Parrott cannon that boasted an accuracy of one and one-half miles. (NPS/ HFCCAC/Hugh Brown)

113

request, but no records or accounts mention any contraband utilized for fortification construction at the Ferry during this period. For ill-disciplined soldiers, however, work on the forts became a punishment. "All enlisted men . . . who have absented themselves without leave or have evaded any duty," ordered a colonel stationed on the heights, "shall upon apprehension be taken under guard to the fortification[s] on Maryland Heights and be there placed and kept at hard labor for a period of not less than five days." Dunn Browne of the 14th Connecticut Infantry, assigned to the detachment guarding "some hundreds of deserters and stragglers," considered the labor "a sort of State's prison business."

The crest of Maryland Heights is denuded of vegetation as seen in this photograph from Pleasant Valley. The B&O Railroad Yard at Sandy Hook, one mile down the Potomac from Harpers Ferry, is visible at far left. (NARA)

Removal of the forests on all three heights became an integral component of the fortification project. Trees impeded the visibility of artillery and infantry and the vegetation offered cover to the enemy. Thus, the timber fell. "It is

an interesting sight to see so many men at work at once felling trees," observed Charles Morse of the 2nd Massachusetts Infantry, while commanding a detachment of 100 tree-choppers on Maryland Heights. "We began our labor at the bottom of a ravine and worked up a steep hill. Sometimes there would be as many as twenty or thirty fine trees falling at once; they reminded me of men falling in battle, that same dead, helpless fall." Details were sent out to burn the fallen timber, but the fresh wood failed to ignite fully. "The men had a free, romantic play-spell one evening in illuminating the mountain side," explained Edmund Brown of the 27th Indiana, "but after the leaves and twigs were consumed the blackened trunks and limbs mostly remained."

By the end of October, the upper third of both Maryland and Loudoun Heights had been denuded, revealing bald, stony crests. Bolivar Heights was stripped naked of vegetation facing westward toward the Shenandoah Valley. "It seems a villainous business, a sacrilege against Nature in her holiest mysteries," recorded Dunn Browne. "But our cannon are pointed in this direction, and whatever interferes with their sweep and destructive efficiency must go on at any cost. The trees must fall that men may the more readily fall if they should come to take their places."

Opposite page, top: *This postwar photograph of the "Stone Fort" shows the perfectly arranged walls and corners of the foundation. After four months of intense labor, the builders abandoned the project, never completing the wooden superstructure.* (NEW HANOVER COUNTY MUSEUM)

Opposite page, bottom: *The massive ruins of the Stone Fort still dominate the crest of Maryland Heights today.* (COURTESY JOHN C. FRYE)

115

Almost Starved

As the politicians and generals argued about strategy during the fall of 1862, nearly 60,000 Union soldiers encircled and encamped at Harpers Ferry—the largest number during the course of the four-year war. The Ferry suddenly ballooned into the second largest city in Virginia—secondary only to war-time Richmond—and the country's fifteenth biggest town based upon the Census of 1860. The army wanted to know who the locals were amongst them. General Orders No. 25 instructed the provost marshal to document all houses, stores, the number of permanent residents, and the number and

THE MAIN STREET, HARPER'S FERRY, VA.—ZOUAVES ON MULES—CONTRABANDS HAULING GUNS—OFFICERS LOUNGING, &C., OCTOBER 16.—SKETCHED BY OUR SPECIAL ARTIST, MR. EDWIN FORBES

description "of all transient residents." The order commanded: "All persons not showing honest occupations or a lawful reason for their presence will be sent across the river." It also warned against corruption: "Gamblers, sharpers, and persons clandestinely introducing liquor into camp will be set at work upon the Fortifications. . . . Women will not be permitted to cross the bridge into Virginia without a pass signed by a General Officer."

Many of the troops at the Ferry had been marching and fighting for six months and their condition was poor. "The whole army had endured a hard campaign," determined Charles Morse, "and must have rest. . . . Neither men nor horses can hold out forever." The fall weather complicated matters. "Men have died—not one, but many," wrote Dunn Browne, "from no

Congestion at the corner of Shenandoah and High Streets as men, material, and mules crowded the streets. (FRANK LESLIE'S WEEKLY, SKETCH BY EDWIN FORBES)

Opposite page: *Military roads on Maryland Heights were well-constructed and remain visible yet today.* (COURTESY DENNIS E. FRYE)

Inset: (NPS/HFCCAC/HUGH BROWN)

other apparent reason than the exposure of sleeping." Cold and uncomfortable, Browne witnessed his men attempt to rest "night after night, week after week, on the ground, without overcoat or blanket, and sometimes without any kind of tent shelter, these cold October nights, on these bare, exposed heights."

Officers complained about the lack of clothing and the inability of the quartermaster to fill requisitions. From his camp on Loudoun Heights, the commander of the 7th Ohio recorded: "There are men in the regiment who have not a shirt to put on, nor can shirts be obtained at present. Many are destitute of articles of clothing." The clothes they did have crawled with vermin. Thousands of men who had been living in close quarters for months—"with very little change of underclothing"—were victims of pests that reproduced at a daily rate of 50 to 60 body-crawling creatures. "At first many tried picking them off," recounted a member of the 4th Maine Light Artillery. "Then boiling our clothes thoroughly was tried, and with constant boiling and watchfulness we succeeded in ridding ourselves of them."

The lack of adequate shelter presented another serious problem. As fall swept through the Harpers Ferry gap, temperatures plummeted at night. The open-air bedding of the summer no longer sufficed. The army provided "shelter tents"—a classic military misnomer—as each soldier was issued only one-half the tent. Even if two halves were buttoned together and suspended over a horizontal pole (resting on forked sticks), both ends of the tent were open, offering virtually no shelter against wind or rain or snow. "Perhaps at no other time was there as much homesickness and discontent as during the few weeks we were at [Harpers Ferry]," summarized the artillery man of the 4th Maine.

"We get about 12 crackers, 2 tablespoons of coffee and 2 of sugar, 2 of salt per day, some times beans, and a piece of pork or fresh beef per day, about half a pound."
—**William Reichard, 128th Pennsylvania Infantry**

The quartermasters did not have a speedy solution to these problems. Supplies were stacked in depots around Washington, but transporting them to the field was a challenge. The B&O Railroad, the primary transporter, did not have enough cars. The C&O Canal's mule-drawn boats were too slow; and wagon trains (one carrying 10,000 shoes) were too long and cumbersome. Loading and unloading conveyances was tedious and time consuming, further restricting the movement of carriers. Complicating matters was the bridge bottleneck at Harpers Ferry, which made it difficult to shuttle supplies across the river. Regardless of these obstacles, supplies rolled forward. On October 16—the third anniversary of John Brown's Raid—10,000 suits; 20,000 blankets; and 10,000 shelter tents were on their way to the Ferry. One week later, the quartermaster department at Harpers Ferry (housed in the old armory buildings) had in its inventory: 24,000 booties; 1,800 blankets; 3,000 stockings; 4,000 infantry trousers; 4,000 infantry overcoats; 7,500 knit jackets; 1,500 cavalry trousers; and 3,000 cavalry overcoats.

Meanwhile, the commissary department distributed food from its depot at the abandoned rifle factory along the Shenandoah. By the third week of October, 40,000 rations arrived each day via the railroad. Charles Morse recorded: "We have a really good cook. . . . He can make good coffee, cook eggs in any way very nicely, and also make pies and puddings; to roast and broil or stew is child's play to him."

Food sometimes arrived spoiled—or worse. "We enjoyed crackers and meat," said a soldier from the 125th Pennsylvania Infantry, but "we preferred to draw them separately and not have the meat cased up in crackers in the shape of live worms." Dunn Browne wrote, "Through the hard rain of last night thousands, and I guess tens of thousands, of bags of oats and corn lay out here under our guard, by the side of the track, soaking through and through! . . . Men, horses, and property of every kind, are all alike neglected, improvidently managed, scattered, and wasted, in this extravagant war."

Camp scenes similar to this one dominated the Harpers Ferry landscape during the Union occupation and revealed the harsh conditions of army life. (LOC/PPOC)

Feeling "almost starved" from the constant eating of salt pork and hard tack, the men would often go foraging. Louis Holt of the 1st Massachusetts Heavy Artillery did a nine-mile jaunt for chow, returning with "three heads of cabbage, a peck of potatoes, two beets, and a haversack of apples." Fruit was a delicacy, as the growing season had mostly ended. Some discovered grapes that made a good jam. Others tasted the paw paw that grew in abundance along the river. "It somewhat resembles the banana, is about half the size, and has about as much taste as a raw pumpkin," mused a soldier in the 4th Maine Battery. "Anything that was green was good, and quantities of them were eaten with a relish." Dunn Browne yearned for the sensation of the kitchen. "I should faint at the very smell of a delicate chicken-broth or a barley-soup, and at the thought of a bowl of bread and milk. Ah, dear me! It is too much. I must change the subject."

On one occasion, food preparation turned dangerous. While encamped on Bolivar Heights, members of the 19th Maine Infantry discovered a heap of old, unexploded cannon shells piled astride the camp. The men knew the fuses and powder could be unstable. One evening while cooking dinner, a thunderstorm blew in consisting of "nine parts wind and one part water." John D. Smith described what happened next. "Well the wind carried the fire and coals into the pile of shells and several of them exploded. Flying fragments were hurled in all directions. . . . Soldiers from the old regiments in the Brigade accused us of trying to cook on the ends of the shells. It was noticed, however, that they were the first to race down the hill to get out of the way of what they imagined to be a flank attack."

Another subject of immense irritation was the absence of mail. "The mail arrangements are very imperfect," wrote William Reichard after receiving no mail for two weeks, and after sending his fourth letter without a response. "I am most sure you at home have written." Four weeks passed before the men in the 14th Connecticut heard from home. When the letters and packages finally began to arrive the "contents have nearly all spoiled by the delay in transmission."

Unhealthy living conditions coupled with poor morale weakened the soldiers' constitutions. "Here the sick are in fearful condition, in every old house and church and hundreds on the ground," discovered Isabella Morrison Fogg while conducting a hospital tour on behalf of the Maine Soldiers' Relief Agency. At Harpers Ferry she found "the stern reality of want, privation and extreme suffering." Sickness and disease decimated the ranks. Pneumonia and tuberculosis collapsed lungs. Diarrhea and dysentery destroyed digestive systems. The bacteria of diphtheria and typhoid fever invaded organs and systems. Disease killed more men than Confederate bullets.

Top: *Nurse Harriett Dada* (MCMOLL/USAMHI)

Bottom: *"Island Hospital" on Virginius Island.* (HFNHP)

More Civil War soldiers died from illness than battlefield bullets or wounds. (THE SOLDIER IN OUR CIVIL WAR, 1885, FRANK LESLIE)

Union surgeons selected an abandoned cotton factory on Virginius Island as the hospital for soldiers stricken with disease. Christened the "Island Hospital," it was one of the tallest buildings in Harpers Ferry, with its four brick stories shadowing the Shenandoah shoreline. Its numerous large windows provided excellent ventilation and light, and its vast floors—now empty of belt machines and spinning wheels—offered the best accommodation for the infirm. "The fourth story was the first to be filled with sick," announced nurse Harriett A. Dada, who arrived from Washington to witness the hospital's opening. "There were iron cots, straw beds, and good new blankets, but pillows, sheets, and even stoves we did not have for some days." As fall grew colder, Nurse Dada recalled "we were obliged to heat bricks and carry them up to those who could not otherwise keep warm."

Nurse Dada was appalled at the condition of the men. "Some of the patients were so covered with vermin that their clothes had to be destroyed." Their hair as well. "The surgeon ordered the heads of several to be shaven, and I made woolen caps for them." Dada observed men so diseased and preyed upon by body pests that they were "quite reduced to skeletons." Visitor Rice C. Bull of the 123rd New York Infantry counted 200 cots per floor. Each floor constituted a ward, "separating the most hopeless from those in less serious condition." All patients were weak and many delirious. "On entering the ward with a basin of water and towel," Dada revealed, "many hands would beckon me to come to them. . . . 'Lady, come here'; or 'Come here; I want a woman to take care of me when I'm

The open slopes of Bolivar Heights became a graveyard for hundreds of Union soldiers who succumbed to disease at Harpers Ferry during the war. Wooden headboards identified most of the deceased who were disinterred and removed to national or private cemeteries in the decade following the war. (HARPER'S WEEKLY)

sick.'" These desperate, often-delusional men knew death was at hand. The need for health care became so demanding that Dada received reinforcements. Nurses Susan Hall, Annie Bell, Sallie Dysart, and Elizabeth Tuttle joined her in November and December since "every floor was filled with very sick patients."

Private Rice Bull assisted a friend who had gangrene in both feet. Bull slept on his blanket on the floor, with his knapsack as his pillow, between cots that were three feet apart. "Nearly every morning from five to ten who had died that night were carried out. . . . We were surrounded by dying men. This was depressing for me but worse for my patient." Bull's friend improved after some toes were amputated, but others were less fortunate. One night, Bull awakened as someone tramped over him. "I heard a crash of glass. . . . I sprang up and saw a man with his head out the window struggling to throw himself out." Private Bull pulled the suicidal man away from the window, but his cuts were deep and he bled so freely that he died before morning. "There was little sleep for anyone that night," claimed Bull. "The horrors soon made me decide that I had no further desire for such service."

The total number of deaths from disease at Harpers Ferry during the fall encampment of 1862 has never been calculated; but with 60,000 men in cramped spaces, with limited shelter and exposure to poor weather, death occurred frequently. Dunn Browne recalled: "Then a brief funeral service, a rough coffin, a shallow grave, and a wooden headboard, for the worn-out soldier of the Union, laid down to his last rest. . . . A true hero, perhaps . . . to lay his life a sacrifice on the altar of his country."

Winter Quarters

As the Union army encircling Harpers Ferry struggled internally, General McClellan continued to gather information on the Confederate whereabouts and intentions. He knew three things for certain: the rejuvenated Confederate army still spread across his front, holding the lower Shenandoah Valley; the administration had vetoed his plan to operate from Harpers Ferry; and President Lincoln was becoming impatient. Subsequently, six weeks after the Harpers Ferry surrender and Union victory at Antietam, McClellan lurched into Virginia, bypassing the Valley, marching south along the east edge of the Blue Ridge. The Confederates likewise moved across the mountain.

Harpers Ferry was not completely vacated. McClellan ordered nearly 12,000 men of the 12th Corps to remain behind to protect the railroad and guard against Confederate river crossings. In essence, it was McClellan's latest version of the Railroad Brigade. The corps spread across the naked crests of Maryland, Loudoun, and Bolivar Heights where they constructed their winter quarters. "Our little group of five built our cabin on the brow of a hill," proclaimed Frederick Wild of Alexander's Baltimore Battery of Light Artillery. "We five lived better then the rest of the boys, because we knew how to utilize the material at hand, that others threw away as useless."

Rice C. Bull of the 123rd New York built a similar log structure on Loudoun Heights. His regiment utilized tent canvas for its hut roofs under orders the canvas "could not be covered with boughs or otherwise to exclude the light." Huts typically were arranged in linear "company streets," although this proved challenging on mountain slopes and narrow crests. The 7th

These log cabins housed the signal corps detachment on Maryland Heights. This drawing was done by Sgt. James Montgomery who was stationed there in the summer of 1864. (HFNHP)

The remains of a chimney hearth on Maryland Heights. Soldiers once gathered around this makeshift fireplace within a log hut for comfort, coffee, and cooking. (COURTESY DENNIS E. FRYE)

Maryland Infantry's Joseph Kirkley wrote of his quarters on Maryland Heights: "After a varied experience of wind, snow, sleet, hail, rain, and mud, the men came to the conclusion that it was nowhere else than up here among these mountains that the weather was made and tried on."

Work on the Maryland Heights fortifications continued into the winter. The War Department agreed to fund $10,000 (20 percent of the original request) of McClellan's grandiose fortress plan. Work progressed steadily, especially at the imposing and massive Stone Fort at the mountain's pinnacle. This blockhouse was designed to repel the Rebels from advancing along the crest of Elk Ridge, as they did against Colonel Miles in September. Although never finished, it remains today as the most conspicuous artifact of the Civil War era. While skilled masons fashioned the Stone Fort, enlisted men continued improvements at the earthen fortifications. Excavation of the earthen storage bunkers for powder and shell near the Naval Battery—picking and shoveling into the rock bed of Maryland Heights—was tough slow labor. "We are building two magazines," Louis Holt informed his sister. "I don't like the job, but I had to take it."

The war's second winter found Harpers Ferry once again desolate. "The ruins of the Government works are a brickyard," noted Charles E. Phelps of the 7th Maryland Infantry. "Churches have become hospitals; gardens and pleasure grounds—graveyards; private residences, barracks and stables. Most of the inhabitants have fled. . . . Only nature is as calm and magnificent as ever."

There was one distraction in the lull of winter: whiskey. "The baking of pies and the smuggling of whiskey were principal employments," joked town resident Joseph Barry, "and these trades continued to flourish at the place all through the war." Commanders strictly forbid the importation of whiskey inside the lines. "Orders were rigid that none should be sold to the men, or even brought over the river," claimed Joseph R. C. Ward of the 106th Pennsylvania during the zenith of the Union occupation. "Yet in spite of all care and precaution, by many ingenious devices it was smuggled and abounded, and those men who wanted it, and who had sufficient money to pay for it, did not have much trouble in getting what they wanted."

The frustrated military used undercover detectives to try to catch the bootleggers. "The result of two or three nights of experimenting in the *roles* of carousers divulged not only the names of dealers, but the place[s] of concealment," Ward recorded. "Some of the dealers had barrels constructed to draw either cider or whiskey; others used, as disguises, boxes of tobacco and other substances not at all suggestive of their real contents. In some places the boards of the floor were removed and 'the stuff' hidden between the joists; in others, concealed in parts of furniture." If caught, offenders were warned and put under surveillance. If the persons persisted, all their wares were seized, they were jailed or banished, or even forced to perform hard labor on the fortifications. Regardless of all efforts, the military never achieved total prohibition. Ward concluded: "The mere fact of it being denied and requiring some strategy to get it no doubt urged some to persist."

On Thanksgiving 1862, the troops enjoyed food if not spirits. From his winter quarters upon Maryland Heights, Warren Holt of the 1st Massachusetts Heavy Artillery shared his day with his sister: "i had my pie for breakfast and turkey for dinner with cranburry sauce and hot potatoes for dinner and bread and butter and pie and plum pudding for supper we had a good time . . . we spent the day in diferent kinds of sport such as pitching quotes and jumping and playing a simple game of cards til dark . . . so the living is not so worse as it might be in the army." Life improved even more for Holt several weeks later with a new addition in camp. "We have got our bake house done and baked the first batch yesterday so now we shal have our soft bread fresh every day . . . we had the bread read hot out of the oven." On Christmas Day Holt wrote, "Our tents crew went to the bake house and got some flower and we made a batch of doughnuts we got the baker to make the dough and I rolled them out and one of the boys fried them and we had a meal of them."

The winter of 1862–63 passed monotonously, but quietly along the Harpers Ferry front. The principal armies were 100 miles away, bogged down in the mud outside Fredericksburg, Virginia. On occasion, the sound of artillery drill shattered the air. When Brigadier General John R. Kenly arrived to command the garrison in December, he was greeted by a salute of 11 cannon. Artilleryman Holt declared: "the Gen was well pleased with the shots that was thrown we are to use the guns every week." Holt's cannon would soon become a necessity for the Federals.

"The baker made a pie apiece for all the company so we lived like kings that day [and] we had baked beef and potatoes and gravy for dinner and the day passed off fine."

—Warren Holt, 1st Massachusetts Heavy Artillery

Winter weather made life and work on Maryland Heights inhospitable and dangerous. Here Harpers Ferry's tallest mountain eerily glows over the frozen Potomac River. (Courtesy Dennis E. Frye)

1863

Higher than the Almighty Intended

Robert E. Lee was pushing north once again. Following successive Confederate victories in the heart of Virginia, General Lee determined in mid-June 1863, to drive the war into Union territory. The Shenandoah Valley became his avenue into the North. Harpers Ferry appeared a likely and vulnerable target. "The air, which for several days past has been heavy and thick with rumor," reflected Joseph Kirkley of the 7th Maryland Infantry, "today crystallized with unmistakable cannonading, which from our elevated position [on Maryland Heights], we could both hear and see." The Confederates had attacked Winchester. Many of the defeated Federals straggled into Harpers Ferry. "Demoralized troops, such as those from Winchester, are not the troops to defend important positions with," wrote Brigadier General Daniel Tyler, the new commander at Harpers Ferry.

The main Confederate column did not pursue the retreating Federals. Instead, the Rebels veered northwest and crossed the Potomac 40 miles upstream from the Ferry. What did this mean? Did Lee plan to swing south toward Washington—placing Harpers Ferry in his crosshairs? Or did he intend to ignore the Ferry, and drive northward instead into Pennsylvania?

"The place must be held," ordered Tyler's department commander from Baltimore. The instructions that followed were reminiscent of those dictated to Colonel Miles nine months earlier. "If you are besieged," contended General-in-Chief Henry Halleck, "you will soon be relieved."

The Camp Hill fortifications surrounding the former armory superintendent's residence were abandoned, rather than tested, during Lee's Gettysburg Campaign. The defense of Maryland Heights proved a better strategic position for Federal commanders, opening the undefended town to temporary Confederate occupation. (FRANK LESLIE'S ILLUSTRATED NEWSPAPER)

General Tyler's response: "I am sending everybody over to Maryland Heights." On June 15, Tyler began an evacuation of the town of Harpers Ferry. "Not a moment was to be lost" in removing tons of quartermaster, commissary, ordnance, and hospital supplies. Every horse and mule team was "put into requisition and used for this purpose," and two days later, officers reported "all the stores safe on the Maryland side."

"The retreats were called skedaddles," wrote Joseph Barry, a Union sympathizer who was also evacuating. "As the enemy approached, a motley crew of fugitives of every shade of color could be seen tramping along the turnpike to Frederick City." Barry had to hurry his departure, for General Tyler ordered the pontoon bridge rendered so that "at any moment" it could swing to the Maryland shore, and he made plans to make the railroad bridge impassable. "These dispositions effectually relieved me from any care on the Virginia side," Tyler reported.

These accomplishments offered little relief for Tyler, however. The bulk of the Confederate army had crossed into Maryland, leaving Tyler to worry about an attack from the north. His existing defenses were designed to stave off assault from the south. Thus, Tyler had to reverse his defenses. Military engineers, fortunately, had considered the prospect of a Confederate attack from the north, so Tyler's men "at once set about carrying out previously well-digested plans." Soldiers who had considered building fortifications a punishment of hard labor vigorously went to work. Stones once considered immobile were moved, hard dirt softened, and cannon were pulled up previously unconquerable heights. Men worked with intensity and purpose. "As the works progressed the spirits of the men revived," reported Tyler's chief engineer after six days of continuous construction. "Instead of gloom and despondency, hope and confidence prevailed."

Most impressive in the transformation was the movement of the guns. "T'were a job not fit for man nor beast!" recorded Sergeant Peter Tower of the 8th New York Heavy Artillery. "First a road had to ascend the steep slopes . . .

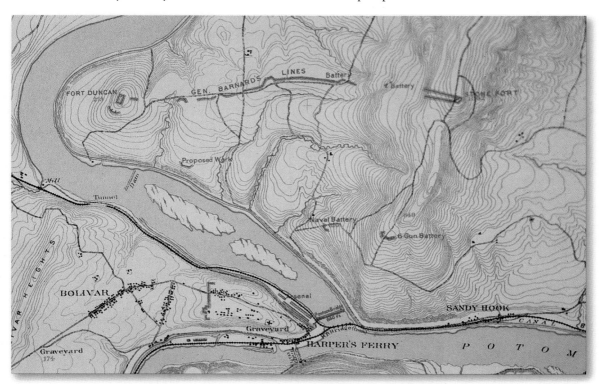

the artillerymen cutting and burning their way through the thick woods. . . . Once the roadway had been wrested from Mother Nature, the New Yorkers then embarked on a worse tussle with the law of gravity—[hoisting cannon] higher than the Almighty intended such ponderous objects to be!" The tube of one iron gun alone weighed nearly five tons (a nine-inch Dahlgren). This was carried more than 1,000 vertical feet. Once the heavy guns were positioned,

*Union engineers designed and strengthened fortifications north of Harpers Ferry during the spring and summer of 1863 in anticipation of future Confederate incursions into the North. They created a fortress stretching two miles from the crest of Maryland Heights to a right-angle bend in the Potomac River. The continuous line of forts and earthworks can be seen on this 1863 military map. (*The Official Military Atlas of the Civil War*)

Opposite page, top: The second Confederate invasion of the North commenced at Williamsport, Maryland. General Lee's plans perplexed the commanders of the U.S. garrison at Harpers Ferry. (THE SOLDIER IN OUR CIVIL WAR, 1885, FRANK LESLIE)

Opposite page, bottom: Brigadier General Daniel Tyler (LOC/PPOC)

> *"Cannot be taken by surprise, and cannot be whipped. Our men are never in better trim for service, confident and impatient."*
>
> —**Joseph Kirkley, 7th Maryland Infantry**

Major General Joseph Hooker (LOC/PPOC)

"cement, rocks, railroad ties, and rails were brought up to strengthen the emplacements. . . . Even drinking water had to be laboriously carried up the Heights."

Summer showers complicated the work. "We could see along the lofty ridge huge guns pointing off over the plains and the white army wagons slowly toiling up its rugged slopes," wrote John Billings of the 10th Massachusetts Battery. "In the afternoon, however, dense clouds rolled over the mountain and drenched everybody and everything with showers of tropical intensity." Billings reported for five consecutive June days he was "alternately cheered by transient sunshine in the morning and copious showers in the afternoon."

As he strengthened his defenses, General Tyler strained to spy the rebels. Nearly a week had passed since the Confederates had crossed the river at Williamsport and Shepherdstown, but the Southerners still had not turned toward Maryland Heights. What were they doing? "The evidence of a heavy force in front of us and around us continues to be visible," expressed Joseph Kirkley. "For several days past, we have seen trains of wagons of almost endless length, creeping along our front from left [south] to right [north]." The telescopes at the Maryland Heights signal station reported Confederate wagon trains stretching from Berryville to Sharpsburg—almost 30 miles.

Tyler's garrison had tripled during the final two weeks of June, now boasting more than 10,500 bluecoats. He also held an advantage that Colonel Miles had lacked—his tie to Washington's reinforcements had not been severed. The previous September, the Confederates interposed between the Ferry and the capital, completely isolating Miles. This time, with the Rebel invasion west of the Blue Ridge, Tyler's communications, supplies, and reinforcements remained intact. The B&O Railroad, heisted by the Confederates in 1862, was still in Federal possession.

With his defenses progressing, adequate troop strength, 33 cannon in position atop the mountain, and his communications connected to his base, General Tyler informed Major General Joseph Hooker, commander of the Union Army of the Potomac: "I expect to hold Maryland Heights against any force that will be brought against it."

The Confederates, however, had Pennsylvania as their target. In the third week of June, Lee's army crossed the Mason-Dixon Line. From his pinnacle, Tyler watched the Confederates vanish further into the northern horizon. "It is apparent that the enemy is moving in force into Pennsylvania," Tyler telegraphed Hooker and General Halleck on June 23. The next day he informed Washington, "It is now almost sure that General Lee is not inclined to attack Maryland Heights."

General Hooker determined a new course of action. With the Rebel threat against Maryland Heights abated—and most of the Confederate army now marching through the Quaker State—Hooker viewed the continued occupation of Maryland Heights useless. On June 27, he informed Halleck: "I find 10,000 men here, in condition to take the field. . . . Here they are of no earthly account. They cannot defend a ford of the river, and, as far as Harper's Ferry is concerned, there is nothing of it." Hooker wanted the Harpers Ferry garrison to join his army at Frederick and assist in the pursuit of Lee into Pennsylvania. Hooker proclaimed if the troops remained on Maryland Heights "they are but a bait for the rebels, should they return."

The War Department refused. "Maryland Heights have always been regarded as an important point to be held by us, and much expense and labor incurred in fortifying them," responded General Halleck. Hooker, already tiring of the administration, was so intransigent on this issue that he resigned—even in the midst of an enemy invasion. President Lincoln immediately named Major General George G. Meade as the new commander of the Army of the Potomac. Halleck granted Meade this unexpected authority: "Harper's Ferry and its garrison are under your direct orders."

Meade wasted no time. Given instructions that he could "diminish or increase" the Harpers Ferry garrison as "circumstances justify," Meade determined to move the troops atop Maryland Heights to Frederick. From here they could protect Meade's rear as his army marched into Pennsylvania, provide a buffer for the defenses of Washington, and ensure the operations of the strategic B&O Railroad. Hence, Meade ordered the evacuation of Maryland Heights on June 28. The order instructed Major General William H. French (who had superceded Tyler) to remove all property from the defenses of Harpers Ferry to Washington, via the C&O Canal.

> *"I cannot approve of their abandonment except in case of absolute necessity."*
> —**General Henry Halleck**

Major General George Gordon Meade (LOC/PPOC)

Next page: *Harpers Ferry from Maryland Heights, depicted in detail by painter William MacLeod in the late spring of 1863. The battery in the foreground is the Naval Battery, overlooking the Potomac. Bolivar Heights appears in the right background, covered with white-canvas tents of a Federal encampment. In the middle ground is Camp Hill, bordered on the left by the Shenandoah River.*

On June 20, 1863—in the midst of the Gettysburg Campaign—the western and north central counties of Virginia (including Jefferson County) broke away from the Old Dominion and were granted U.S. statehood. Harpers Ferry now technically belonged to the Union. The Confederates had left Virginia when they crossed north of the Potomac, but when they retreated south after their defeat at Gettysburg, they entered West Virginia. (ACCESSION #54.2, ARTIST WILLIAM DOUGLAS MACLEOD, *MARYLAND HEIGHTS: SIEGE OF HARPERS FERRY*, 1863, OIL ON CANVAS, 30 X 44 INCHES, COURTESY OF CORCORAN GALLERY OF ART, WASHINGTON D.C., GIFT OF GENEVIEVE PLUMMER.)

"A hasty evacuation of a position which so much care had been taken to fortify," wrote Joseph Kirkley. General French delayed the tedious and laborious operation until the evening of June 29, due to "the limited number of wagons at the post." The evacuation continued for 17 hours, hauling guns and ordnance and provisions down the mountain to waiting canal boats at Sandy Hook. The 1st Massachusetts Heavy Artillery—that had constructed 12 magazines and four batteries on the mountain's defenses, and hauled up 35 cannon and 220 tons of ammunition since the previous October—directed the disassembling of the artillery. Much of it transpired in darkness, and most of it in rain. As Kirkley described: "Rain was pouring in sheets and the mountain roads were becoming beds of torrents."

The 7th Maryland stalled just below the "Buzzard Battery," where the 8th New York Heavy Artillery was defusing 100-pound shells. As the men waited a thunderous roar suddenly shook the earth. "An accidental explosion!" Kirkley surmised. In seconds, "fragments of shell, rock, and timber" hailed down

Earthen magazines similar to this stored gunpowder and cannon shells in underground bunkers. During the rapid evacuation of Maryland Heights, a magazine exploded, killing several Union soldiers. (NPS/ HFCCAC/Hugh Brown)

on the Marylanders. "And shocking to add, human bodies also . . . limbs without bodies and bodies [falling] at my very feet." Soon Kirkley witnessed the wounded and dead, "horribly mutilated, borne through our ranks on stretchers." Kirkley later learned that nine were killed and 12 wounded by the accident. John Billings of the 10th Massachusetts Battery reported the explosion occurred when "someone with more zeal than discretion struck a percussion shell with an axe." When the shell exploded, it set ablaze an adjoining ordnance magazine, and this in turn blew up, resulting in the heavy and gruesome casualties. No less than three explosions occurred during the rapid withdrawal, but they were not as deadly.

Not all the cannon, ordnance, and provisions were removed. Several of the heavy guns were left in place to cover the retreat and protect the canal boat convoy heading downstream toward Washington. At 10:30 p.m. on July 1—the first day of the Battle of Gettysburg—the last remaining artillerymen on Maryland Heights learned the troops and boats were out of range of their guns. Executing their final orders, they "spiked" (disabled) the remaining cannon, and pushed them from their carriages and down the steep mountain slope. All remaining ammunition was destroyed. The last evacuees ensured the Rebels would not retrieve their guns.

Very few Confederates were in the area. Virtually every man in Robert E. Lee's Army of Northern Virginia was north of the Mason-Dixon Line with the exception of one regiment, the 12th Virginia Cavalry. Comprised of local men from the lower Valley (including three companies from Jefferson County), these several hundred horsemen were instructed to remain in the Valley to recruit for their ranks and to help protect Lee's line of supply. Squadrons first appeared near Harpers Ferry during the final week of June, where they surprised and captured a Federal cavalry detachment on June 30. But the Confederates arrived too late to interfere with the evacuation. They found a mostly empty town, void of population and provisions. With Maryland Heights abandoned, 12th Cavalry squadrons roamed the town freely, even crossing the B&O Railroad bridge which was left intact.

An Ill-Planned Evacuation

Following the Confederate defeat at Gettysburg the first week of July, General Lee retreated rapidly toward the Potomac. However, days of torrential rain had flooded the river. A prompt return to the Confederacy was impossible. This afforded General Meade an opportunity to trap Lee in Maryland, beat him across the river, swing in behind the Confederates, and slice their line of retreat. The Union commander recognized a crossing at Harpers Ferry as his best chance. Just two days after the Battle of Gettysburg had ended, Meade urgently directed his pontoon chief to, "Put your [pontoon] bridge trains and troops in motion at once for Harper's Ferry." To ensure Lee could not utilize the bulwark of Maryland Heights for his own protection, and to prevent Lee's army from retreating to Virginia via Harpers Ferry, Union authorities also ordered the seizure of Maryland Heights. The army immediately dispatched a Maryland brigade of 1,700 men from Frederick. On July 7—only six days after the previous evacuation—the Stars and Stripes again waved atop the pinnacle.

Meade did not know it, but he already had a bridge in place at the Ferry: the B&O Railroad bridge. For some inexplicable reason, the Confederates had not destroyed it. Union cavalry could cross here and sever the enemy's retreat. Misfortune struck, however, at the hands of allies.

On July 5, General French—unaware of Meade's desire to cross at Harpers Ferry—ordered Union cavalry to blow both ends of the bridge to keep it out of Rebel possession. When Meade's chief of staff learned of the untimely destruction, he reported: "General French [had] destroyed the use of the

Armored rail cars equipped with cannon, similar to the one illustrated here, arrived opposite Harpers Ferry at the conclusion of the Gettysburg Campaign. They were intended to assist with protection of the B&O Railroad during its reconstruction, but witnessed little activity. (THE SOLDIER IN OUR CIVIL WAR)

Harper's Ferry railroad bridge so that we cannot throw any cavalry across." Thus, the Federals lost an extraordinary opportunity to beat Lee across the Potomac and disrupt or even deter the Confederate escape back to Virginia.

John R. Meigs was not deterred, however. The enterprising military engineer and recent graduate of West Point arrived at Harpers Ferry on July 7 with five ironclad railroad cars mounted with cannon, that Meigs believed could withstand enemy musketry and even cannonballs. "I am not afraid of the heavy masses of the enemy, provided they cannot get heavy artillery to work at me." Upon arrival, Meigs immediately "shelled the rebel bushwackers quiet" on the Harpers Ferry side. He then contemplated a strategy to cut off Lee. Knowing no time could be lost, he boldly proposed *his* supervision of a corps of railroad men for the reconstruction of the bridge. The military promptly thwarted the ambitious lieutenant, warning: "You must be cautious as well as active." The rail bridge, consequently, did not reopen for nearly two weeks.

"Dried apples, hard tack, rice and sugar, all mixed and jumbled together, lay in heaps, from two to three feet deep. The farmers from the near country have take[n] away large supply for present and future wants," reported Lieutenant Colonel William Lincoln when his 34th Massachusetts Infantry regiment arrived on Maryland Heights the second week of July. Lincoln also noticed military items in disarray, including piles of tents, as good as new, "save that each has been slit once from top to bottom . . . heaps of Springfield muskets, many of them with broken stocks indeed, but many entirely uninjured. Everything shows a hurried, and ill-considered, and ill-planned evacuation."

Corporal Charles Moulton concurred. "It seems wicked to see the enormous quantities of provisions destroyed and laying wasting all around the lots." The mud of Maryland Heights, however, impressed Moulton as even more onerous. "The mud was two feet deep in places, from which a most nauseous, putrefied scent arose, nearly smothering us and forcibly reminding one of the 'Valley of Death.'" Moulton, who had been encamped with his 34th Massachusetts near the capital for months, noted the change in his quality of life. "It seems rather tough to be here lying in shelter tents in the mud and wet, with scarcely anything to eat, after faring so 'top shelf' in Washington." Further aggravating Moulton was the sudden hard labor. "We drew two guns some two miles up a steep hill into Fort Duncan through the rain and mud and got completely drenched through the operation." As the army began returning the heavy artillery ordnance to the fortress of Maryland Heights, Moulton reflected on the difficulty of this work. "The guns each weighed 4,240 lbs. and it required 10 horses and 100 men at each one. If people up North still fret and wonder and blow because the army doesn't move rapidly, I would advise them to just come down and take a look at the mere 'trifle' we undertook this morning and they will 'dry up.'"

The big guns would not be necessary, at least at present. As the Potomac receded, General Lee and the Confederate army continued their retreat. This prompted the Federals to seize Harpers Ferry and erect a new pontoon bridge to affect a crossing. The 34th Massachusetts received orders to lead the way and provide cover for the operation. Two boats soon splashed into the water carrying armed men led by the regiment's Colonel William Wells. "The Colonel was in the first boat with a big long oar telling the boys to do as well as they knew how," wrote Private Horace Ball. When the boats landed, the Yankees were greeted by "something standing in the road, looking like a piece of artillery pointed at us." Corporal Moulton wondered "why it didn't blaze away at us. We soon found out its real nature in the shape of a stove-pipe mounted on two wheels, thus representing one of the Reb's Quaker guns, with which they intended to scare us." Private Ball recalled: "What few rebels there was left double quick; there was nothing there but a picket." Moulton soon boasted to his hometown newspaper that the 34th Massachusetts "had the honor of being the first Union regiment that set its foot upon the 'sacred soil' after the recent retreat of Lee from Pennsylvania."

Federal engineers rapidly constructed the pontoon bridge the afternoon of July 14. Over the next five days, nearly 40,000 men in three different corps in the Army of the Potomac crossed the pontoons at Harpers Ferry in pursuit of Lee's withdrawing army. No battles occurred in the Valley, however; and the two armies drifted away into central Virginia where they remained for the next nine months.

> **"What a frightful waste of property attended the evacuation of this position!"**
>
> —Lieutenant Colonel William Lincoln, 34th Massachusetts Infantry

A wooden canteen, typical of the period. (NPS/DIP)

Tired of War

Charles Moulton was not impressed with his first glimpse at Harpers Ferry. "Splendid landscape scenery for the artist—but now all is desolated and utter ruin; war has had its effect and laid every thing waste and barren . . . the entire place is not actually worth $10." However, after a month of Federal reoccupation and his encampment at Camp Hill on the grounds of the old armory superintendent's quarters, Moulton's attitude changed. "Harper's Ferry bears quite a lively aspect, considering war times. Among the institutions established are a post and express office, Government hospital, bakery and Commissary storehouse." Moulton also observed an influx of citizens "flocking into the place in large numbers, now that they can rest assured of safety."

Among the returning civilians was Abba Goddard, Matron of the Clayton General Hospital nine months before. Brigadier General Henry H. Lockwood, commandant of the Maryland Brigade, had commandeered the old hospital site for his headquarters; and the Matron was stunned when she paid a visit. "The beautiful trees that shaded the building have been cut down, and even the cherry trees under which we buried our dead after the [September 1862] battle have been destroyed. . . . Only the [grave] mound is left and soon that will gradually disappear, and the only record the gallant dead will possess will be existing in devastated households and broken hearts." Mrs. Goddard also voiced her displeasure at locals who had plundered Uncle Sam's stores during the recent evacuation, securing barrels of flour, sugar, and coffee. "About half the citizens are clad in garments made up from hospital goods. Dear me! Wouldn't I have rejoiced at the opportunity to gather up the secreted stores. But I am not a '[wo]man having authority' and therefore can only look."

The 34th Massachusetts Infantry also had its encounters with the local population. The regiment had a reputation for stealing, especially after soldiers had swiped boards, doors, and windows from some of the old abandoned government buildings to construct floors and doors in its Camp Hill tents. General Lockwood objected, ordering a thorough examination of the camp and the arrest and confinement of "the occupants of any tent in which any such government property may be found." Word of this discipline spread, and the men of the 34th soon were blamed for any disappearance.

Illness and disease, particularly smallpox, became a serious matter with the reintroduction of garrison life into Harpers Ferry. "Everybody here is about 'skeered' to death just now in regard to the small pox," Charles Moulton discerned, "which is raging to a considerable extent." The disease first appeared among the town's black population, but was spreading. To abet its diffusion, a patrol of 19 men who had had the disease was formed "whose business it is to visit every house and search all rooms, and upon all cases of the loathsome disease to send them to headquarters, where the patients must be removed at once." Because the disease was so infectious, a separate hospital "pest house" was established in Bolivar. Moulton himself contracted a mild case of the disease, suffering from acute fever, chills, itching, nausea, and red blotches over the skin.

Occasionally, the war offered a respite from so much hardship. On Thanksgiving Day, 1863, Joseph F. Ward admitted to his sister: "I did not do much of anything but eat." Ward was a member of the 34th Massachusetts' brass band, and he and his fellow musicians feasted on goodies sent from home, including "three large turkeys, four or five chickens and pies, cakes, cheese, [and] apples innumerable." Ward noted one of the band members was a fine cook who prepared a nice large plum pudding, "I believe as good as I ever eat."

"Festoons of evergreen were gracefully and fantastically entwined about every pillar and projection of the architecture, while here and there stacks of polished muskets intervened, the brilliancy of which in the bright lamp light, formed a beautiful contrast with the dark evergreen background."

—**Charles Moulton, 34th Massachusetts**

That evening, a "Grand Military Ball," hosted by the officers of the 34th Massachusetts, enlivened the old paymaster's quarters, now coined the Lockwood House. No less than three generals attended, along with wives and daughters of officers and "all the principal ladies in and about the town." Supper, provided by a fashionable caterer from Baltimore, featured "three varieties of cake, piled upon broad, shallow, white crockery dishes, sweet water grapes, carefully picked from the stem, stewed oysters, and a whitish, lumpy looking compound, unrecognizable by taste, but announced as chicken salad." Beautiful decorations adorned the interior. Particularly admired was a chandelier, "made by a circle of bayonets," suspended from the hallway ceiling. Another proud attraction was a rack of guns comprised of "the best gun from each company." The brass band of the 34th Infantry serenaded the audience, and "the music could not be excelled." Festivities continued until "reveille from the bugles in the camp [brought] the signal to disperse." The sergeants hosted their own ball a few days later, followed by yet another one the week after Thanksgiving, held by the local residents in the Factory Hospital buildings on Virginius Island.

Invitation to the ball, printed on a military press at Harpers Ferry. (HFNHP)

GRAND MILITARY BALL,
BY THE
OFFICERS OF THE 34th MASSACHUSETTS INFANTRY,
ON THANKSGIVING EVENING,
NOVEMBER 26th, 1863,
AT THE BUILDING RECENTLY USED BY GEN. LOCKWOOD AS HEAD-QUARTERS.

COMMITTEE OF ARRANGEMENTS:

Capt. Wm. B. Bacon,
Lieut. George Macomber,

Capt. H. P. Fox,
Lieut. Levi Lincoln, Jr.

Respectfully invited to attend.

Harper's Ferry, Va., Nov. 23, 1863.

Such reverie attracted considerable attention, but not as much as the deluge of Confederate deserters walking into Union lines at Harpers Ferry. "Deserters from the Rebels come in daily, averaging from six to twelve in number, and one day . . . amounting to thirty," Colonel Lincoln observed. The Confederate loss at Gettysburg had dampened the war enthusiasm of many Southern soldiers. "I can not say that I am enjoying myself at all

"All quiet along the Potomac to-night—
No sound save the rush of the river;
While soft falls the dew on the face of the dead—
The picket's off duty forever."

at this time," wrote Daniel Sheetz of the 2nd Virginia Infantry two weeks after the defeat at Gettysburg. "I am too much waried down from the march that we had in the yankee states . . . it was the hardest times that we had since the war." Sheetz summarized the dejection of many Confederate soldiers: "I was in good hopes that the war would soon be over, but it don't look much like it at this time." Nearly one-third of the 2nd Virginia deserted in the two weeks after Lee's reentry into Virginia.

Now assigned as a clerk in the provost office—where the deserters were processed—Charles Moulton recorded the phenomenon. "Many deserters come in and give themselves up, take the oath [of allegiance to the United States] and are sent the other side of the Potomac to remain during the war." Moulton explained their reason: "They are tired of the war and have got enough of fighting." Moulton witnessed some deserters "bring their whole family with them." During the first quarter of 1864, Moulton counted 2,500 deserters in his military department. Once delivered into Maryland, they could not return south until the war had ended, under penalty of being a spy.

These are the final lines of the poem "The Picket Guard" written by Ethel Lynn Beers in 1861 for Harper's Weekly. *The poem was later set to music and called "All Quiet Along the Potomac Tonight." In this illustration Alfred R. Waud, one of the Civil War's most famous illustrators, captured the gloomy mood of the Potomac River carving its way through the Harpers Ferry gap.* (LOC)

The Gray Ghost

With the exception of deserters, few Confederate soldiers could be found in the Harpers Ferry district during the winter of 1863–1864. But one who did roam the region brought instant fear to the lips of every Federal. John Singleton Mosby was the most successful and pervasive Rebel guerilla.

Colonel John Singleton Mosby (LOC/PPOC)

"To my mind Mosby was the ideal fighting man, from the tip of his plume to the rowel of his spur," wrote John Munson, a member of Mosby's 43rd Virginia Cavalry. "Stories of his wonderful achievements came into Richmond from every direction. Joan of Arc never felt the call to go to battle any stronger than I felt it to join Mosby."

Rumors of Mosby's attacks and escapes created a Mosby mythology and made him a hated nemesis of the Federals. Yet Colonel Henry Cole and his 1st Maryland Potomac Home Brigade Cavalry refused to shrink before the legend, and made repeated attempts to "bag" Mosby and his men.

Determined to end Cole's career, "The Gray Ghost" gathered 110 guerillas one week after New Year's 1864 and rode—in near zero degrees and through one foot of snow—to Cole's camp along the Hillsboro road at the base of Loudoun Heights. Cole's nearest support was almost two miles away at the Ferry. "While riding, we would put the reins in our mouth and our hands under the saddle blanket, next to the horses' skins, to keep from being frozen," recorded raider J. Marshall Crawford. About a mile and a half south of Cole's position, the command split. One party straddled Short Hill Mountain, heading for the Potomac, and the other remained astride the Hillsboro road. The river squadron encountered a rough ride, as John Scott described, "ascending on our route a wooded cliff, which could only be done by leading our horses, and grasping in our ascent the thick bushes." Once upon the crest, Crawford realized "we could touch the tents with our pistols."

Silently, Mosby made dispositions to capture Cole and launch the assault. "Everything so far seemed to promise success to the enterprise," Crawford predicted, "and render it the most brilliant affair of the war." The clock ticked near 3:00 a.m., Sunday, January 10. Suddenly, something went wrong. Partisans from the river route galloped into the enemy camp before the signal. The remainder of Mosby's men, thinking them to be Yankees, opened fire, killing or wounding their own troops. These errant shots awakened Cole's bluecoats, and a close-order, hand-to-hand violent fight followed.

"No one who has not experienced a night attack from an enemy can form the slightest conception of the feelings of one awakened in the dead of night with the din of shots and yells coming from those thirsting for your blood," exclaimed C. Armour Newcomer of Cole's Cavalry. "Each and every man in that attack, for the time, was an assassin. . . . It was hand-to-hand, and so dark, you could not see the face of the enemy you were shooting. It was a perfect hell!"

Amid the chaos, a signal gun sounded the alarm at the Ferry. In 10 minutes the 34th Massachusetts Infantry was double-quicking two miles toward the turmoil. "Kept it up till we got there and then there was not a reb to be seen," reported Horace Ball. Mosby had heard the signal gun too, and with his command in shatters he ordered a retreat. The fight lasted less than 15 minutes. "We brought off ten prisoners and forty-five horses—a poor compensation for the grievous loss the battalion had sustained," wrote John Scott. Killed were two captains and two lieutenants, invaluable leaders of Mosby's command, along with about a half dozen other Confederate casualties. It was John Mosby's worst defeat of the Civil War.

Attack by Mosby's guerillas as depicted by Harper's Weekly. (LOC)

1864—1865

Garrison for the Conqueror

ffairs at Harpers Ferry during the winter of 1863–1864 were "assuming a rather dull and monotonous aspect," for provost marshal clerk Charles Moulton. Perhaps the principal excitement was enforcing martial law throughout the district, primarily through the issuance of military passes. "According to military law, we must be very particular to whom we grant passes and have to be rather inquisitive, asking all sorts of curious questions." What is your business? Where are you going? Whom are you going to see? Moulton noted that all requestors must take the Oath of Allegiance to the United States or show proof that they had sworn allegiance previously. Once a pass was issued, it required a signature on the back. "But no one-half of them can do this," Moulton noted. "In this case we have to do it for them and go through the cross 'his or her mark' plan." The educated Moulton was "surprised to find the majority of the people so ignorant as they really are. Some of them are very smart, pretty looking young ladies, dressed in fine style, but cannot write a word."

To ensure no counterfeiting or transfer of passes, each pass contained "the full, correct description of the person to whom it is granted." Moulton particularly enjoyed this aspect of his job, "on account of the fine chances afforded to see the pretty girls." He delighted at the opportunity to "gaze at their smiling countenances. . . . We have to ask them their age, which is a very delicate question to ask young ladys [sic]."

Not many passes were issued the third week of April when the lower town of Harpers Ferry was under water.

The former smith and forging shop at the armory became the nucleus of Sheridan's supply depot. An average supply train included 1,000 wagons, hitched to 6,000 mules—and would stretch for more than 10 miles. (LOC, SKETCH BY A. R. WAUD)

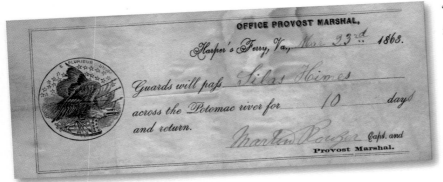

The military pass controlled all civilian movement. (HFNHP)

The military pass controlled all civilian movement. (HFNHP)

"Shenandoah Street was flooded and for a few days was a miniature Potomac branch," Moulton wrote. Thirty-feet of one of the spans on the iron railroad bridge washed away on April 10, even though five 40-ton coal cars weighted it down, sending all into the torrent "with a crash." The current proved too swift to maintain the pontoon bridge as well, so it was taken up, cutting all communication with the Maryland shore. "The mail was drawn across in a basket attached to a rope pulley and a squad of the pontoon boys realized quite a nice little sum in moving over people in a boat, one dollar per ticket." Since the B&O was engaged in transporting large bodies of troops at the time, it built a temporary pedestrian footbridge suspended from a five-inch wire cable. Vice President Hannibal Hamlin, his wife, and a group of U.S. senators were the first to cross the temporary structure en route back to Washington.

The new railroad bridge reopened to train traffic on April 18, but survived less than one month. The Potomac rose so rapidly in mid-May that the pontoons could not be removed. The boat bridge collapsed, sending many of the boats ramming into the tenuous piers where they lodged with accumulating driftwood. This proved too much for the fragile trestles, and on May 16, the bridge collapsed. The B&O attempted the cable approach once more, but "the men in charge of the boat were compelled, from the condition of the current, to throw the cable into the river to save themselves." Work on new trestles began on May 19. Just two days later—in a record 48 hours—trains were crossing the bridge.

When the bridge was operational, many passenger trains passed through Harpers Ferry. Anyone detraining, in addition to acquiring a pass from the provost marshal, had all baggage and possessions searched. "If anything contraband is found in them, the whole lot is confiscated," Charles Moulton pronounced. All mail entering and leaving Harpers Ferry also passed through the provost office, where it was scrutinized carefully for anti-Union rhetoric. One day alone, Moulton read 300 letters. "All letters must go through an examination before they are permitted to reach their destination . . . very frequently we tear up a long affectionate missive on account of its disloyal sentiments."

The provost marshal dealt with three types of violators: civilians, deserters, and soldiers. Union deserters were not too frequent, and their stay was usually short, as they often were forwarded elsewhere for court-martial,

"[We] stare at them to ascertain the color of their eyes, hair, and complexion, and ask their height and if they don't know, why they must be measured. Many a pretty girl blushes through this apparent impudence."

—Charles Moulton, 34th Massachusetts

146

No known photographs depict flood conditions in Harpers Ferry during the war. Flood levels were lower than in this 1889 deluge, but still rampaging and destructive. (HFNHP)

hard labor, or prison. Frequent infractions included drunkenness, stealing, and falling asleep at post. This last transgression amounted to a crime against fellow soldiers—especially with the constant threat of Confederate guerillas—and it always met with severe punishment.

Civilians could be confined in prison for a multitude of sins, including prostitution, selling liquor, illegal transport of goods, harboring guerillas, assisting the enemy, or—worst of all—spying. Anyone accused as a spy was shipped to Fort McHenry in Baltimore and held there unconditionally, usually without opportunity for a trial. Just the charge of "suspicious character" landed people in the provost's jail. Adeleine Osborne was imprisoned for "rebellious letters taken from Harper's Ferry Post Office." Bushrod Taylor was seized for "blacksmithing for the rebels." William Rigsby was imprisoned for "making rebel uniforms." George Buckannon's crimes were "seduction and obtaining a pass under false pretenses."

The jailhouse of choice at the Ferry had become the armory paymaster's office, located adjacent to the John Brown Fort. It was not a pleasant place. During one inspection, 40 prisoners were confined in an 18-by-18-foot room. There was no separation of the incarcerated. Civilians, Union soldiers, and Confederate POWs were jumbled together. Two separate back rooms, empty at the time of the inspection, were "filthy, dark and badly ventilated & covered with human _____." The inspector found the paymaster's vault, known as "the dungeon," also empty, but built to be "burglar, air, and light proof." A

The John Brown Fort (front) served as a prison at various times throughout the war, as did the adjoining paymaster's office. Here they appear 25 years after the war. A wall still separates the grounds of the old armory from Potomac Street; remains of the smith and forging shop appear in the background. (HFNHP)

148

lieutenant of the guard informed the inspector that he recently had "put 7 Negroes in the dungeon one night and that 'they were sick enough in the morning.' It is marvelous they survived the incarceration." Regarding the two back rooms and the vault, the inspector reported: "I must condemn unqualifiedly."

The New Students

In the spring of 1864, 65 former slaves, now living behind Union lines, began to receive their first formal education in Harpers Ferry. Enrolled in day and night schools sponsored by a philanthropic New England organization called the American Missionary Association, eager African American students studied the *Bible,* learning how to read and write under the guidance of missionary teachers W. W. Wheeler and his wife Ellen. When the Wheelers first arrived the "military authorities seemed little disposed to grant us the facilities which the Government usually furnishes." The missionaries soon discovered a patron in Major General Franz Sigel, department commander,

Missionaries from the North established schools for former slaves while the war still raged. (HARPER'S WEEKLY)

former New York City schoolteacher, and an ardent abolitionist. Sigel promptly granted their requests for rations, quarters, and classroom materials. The Wheelers reported "we feel ourselves greatly honored, in being permitted to open a school for those very ones for whom he died, within a few rods of the Armory buildings in which [John Brown] took refuge."

Wheeler marveled at the patience, spirit, and industriousness of his new pupils. "Contrary to the false statements of their enemies they are abundantly capable of taking care of themselves." He met enterprising blacks that had saved considerable sums of money through an allowable practice in the slave system of "hiring out your time." Wheeler was particularly impressed with the generosity his students extended to a white soldier who had been a prisoner for more than nine months. He was destitute, with almost no clothing, no shoes, no money, and nearly blind. "I laid his case before the school, and though but few were there and not well prepared for it they gave him $4.15. . . . Would a white school have given it to a colored soldier?"

Though optimistic about his students' futures, Wheeler and his school experienced the realism of the present. "We find much opposition manifested by the citizens of the place, though they are powerless to do us harm . . . our schoolhouse is stoned, the window glass is broken and abusive epithets are bestowed upon us." On June 22, Wheeler recounted one tragic occurrence:

German-born Franz Sigel, who commanded the Shenandoah Valley in the spring of 1864, strongly supported the education of former slaves. (LOC/PPOC)

> The opposition to the school among the white citizens seems to have been increasing of late & Sunday night it culminated in an outbreak. One of the little black boys was sitting listening to the band playing when a white boy came up & spit in his face and upon his clothes and began to shake a stick at him & finally to strike at him with it when he took it away from him. Other white boys came up & he ran when they began throwing stones the guard encouraging them on. They ran down to the church where the colored people were assembling. Here stones were thrown freely by the white boys & I believe a few by the blacks. But a black man made them stop. I heard the noise & came to the door when a stone came by me into the church. I called the boys in & the white boys kept hallowing around the house till meeting was over when they began throwing stones again. They hurt one woman considerably and struck a little girl in the face. The next day I had to call the boys in from recess because the white boys were stoning them.
>
> I went to the Provost Marshall & gave the names of several of the rioters & he had them arrested—but his sargeant let them go & arrested two colored boys & blindfolded one & shot gun caps at him going through the farce of a military execution. This was done without the order of the Provost Marshall—but I have seen him since & he 'cares for none of these things.' The colored people are subjected to almost daily insult from the soldiers. I saw one young woman with her dress skirt torn half off by a drunken soldier & another I saw struck in her face by another soldier also drunk. The colored people bear these insults with very commendable patience scarcely ever returning an insult—unless it be among the boys who sometimes show a degree of spirit worthy of the superior race.

(LOC)

Now what do we do if these persecutions continue & the military use its power in encouraging them? I wish you would tell us. A Methodist Brother has come here from the North to build up the Methodist Churches on a 'union basis.' He has proposed to some of the white members to hold meetings in our church but they utterly refuse to attend meetings in that N . . . r house. I must say that I think the 'Union' 'in the basis' is rather small.

Despite the intimidation, violence, and lack of support from the Northern military authorities and soldiers, Ellen Wheeler filed an optimistic report on July 1. The average class size had grown to 40, although "the measles coming among the children" detained many from attending. School began each morning at 7:30 a.m. in order to "close and return home before the greatest heat of the day." Writing, Mental Arithmetic, and Geography were the classes, but "nothing gives me so much pleasure as the thought of those texts of scripture of which they have now learned at least twenty." Mr. Wheeler wrote on the same day that his attendance at night school was smaller. He determined nightly punctuality could not be expected for "men who work hard all day [for the government] as teamsters, in the 'forage house' handling heavy boxes or at the anvil; and women [who] lard all day over the washtub or over the stove in the kitchen."

As Mrs. Wheeler prepared the final paragraph of her report, she noticed the calendar. "Mr. Wheeler explained to the class, today, the reason for the observation of the approaching fourth of July, and also told them something of their 'Independence day' January 1, 1863. . . . We should be glad to observe the 4th July, in our school, but we think it hardly safe for the colored people to meet on that day, with the present state of feeling toward them, in the town."

Matters did quickly worsen. The Rebel army was marching toward Harpers Ferry.

Lieutenant General Jubal A. Early (LOC/PPOC)

The Yearly Skedaddle

Action around Harpers Ferry had been subdued for months. Union forces supplied from the town were operating deep in Confederate territory in the upper Shenandoah Valley, more than 100 miles distant. The two major armies battled each other in little known places in Virginia like The Wilderness, Spotsylvania, and Cold Harbor. Lieutenant General Ulysses S. Grant had taken command of the Union armies in the spring of 1864, and "Unconditional Surrender" Grant was smashing his way toward Richmond. By early summer, the combatants were bogged down in trench warfare near Petersburg, Virginia. General

Lee, desperate to break the siege, dispatched Lieutenant General Jubal A. Early with about 14,000 men on a diversion mission to threaten Washington. Early chose the Shenandoah Valley as his portal to the capital—and Harpers Ferry stood in his way.

"The enemy are approaching, by way of Charlestown, in heavy force," pronounced Brigadier General Max Weber just before noon on July 4. The current base commander at the Ferry informed General-in-Chief Henry Halleck in Washington that if reinforcements did not arrive, "I must leave the town, but shall hold Maryland Heights at all hazards."

"It was time for the yearly 'skedaddle,'" announced provost clerk Charles Moulton as he watched the quartermaster, commissary, and ordnance supplies hurried across the Potomac for safekeeping. Indeed, one year had passed since the last evacuation during the Gettysburg Campaign. "At no time during the war was there as deep

Major General Henry W. Halleck (LOC/PPOC)

a gloom on Harper's Ferry as on that anniversary of the birth of our nation," recorded town resident Joseph Barry. "The people had entertained the fond hope that the war was nearly over." Confederates soon approached Bolivar Heights, pressing against the Federal left along the Shenandoah, employing tactics similar to Stonewall Jackson's during the great siege in 1862. Heavy skirmishing occurred. General Weber pulled his forces back into the defenses of Camp Hill—the same earthworks Colonel Miles had constructed two years earlier. With Bolivar abandoned, the Confederates pressed forward with their sharpshooters, hiding themselves "in the houses and behind fences and in the orchards and everywhere to keep out of sight and pick off our men." The chief of artillery, poised upon Maryland Heights, inquired, "Will it do to throw shell into or over Bolivar? The d—d town is full of rebels." The artillery opened fire, blasting Bolivar Heights. "Every house in Bolivar was damaged to a more or less extent," Moulton wrote. "It is a singular fact that every house that was struck by our shells was the property of Union persons, which plainly shows that they had been pointed out to the Rebs by their sympathizing friends."

During the early evening of July 4, General Weber abandoned Harpers Ferry and retired to the defenses of Maryland Heights, where he had 30 days rations in storage. Federal troops removed the pontoon bridge and set the B&O Railroad bridge on fire. "It was a grand and sublime sight to look over into the Ferry and see the flames shooting upwards from all parts and directions of the old town . . . and listen to the deep booming of the shells over our heads all through the night," observed Charles Moulton from his new perch on Maryland Heights.

> *"Everything should be prepared for the defense of your works, and the first man who proposes a surrender or retreats should be hung."*
>
> **—Henry W. Halleck**

The next morning the signal station on the Heights spied long Confederate columns crossing the Potomac about eight miles upriver near Shepherdstown. The Southerners crossed continuously for 40 hours. Then the Rebels turned south, adhering to Confederate General Early's definitive directive: "Compel the evacuation of Maryland Heights.... Promptness and dispatch are absolutely necessary."

General Franz Sigel, meanwhile, had arrived with his command. Additional reinforcements had hurried from Washington, bolstering the Union troop strength on Maryland Heights to about 10,000 men. Authorities in Washington, meanwhile, began to panic. "We have almost nothing in Baltimore and Washington, except militia, and considerable alarm has been created," Halleck informed General Grant. If the Maryland Heights position collapsed, Washington was vulnerable. Halleck urged Grant to send someone to the empty defenses of the U.S. capital.

As Sigel watched the Confederate army approach from the Maryland side of the Potomac, he became annoyed by Rebel sharpshooters in

Harpers Ferry. They were posted along the armory river wall and the B&O trestles, firing across the Potomac into Union supply trains coming up from Sandy Hook. Sigel "notified citizens to vacate houses, as he would shell the town."

"The roar of the cannon is continuous, and there is nothing to be done but to endure it and thank God that the balls and shell whiz by high enough to leave them unscathed. . . . It is a tedious, irksome, weary time of watching and of dread. When will it cease?"

—**Annie Marmion**

Grade-schooler Annie Marmion never forgot the next two days. "The little Village of Harper's Ferry had its worst experience of a Bombardment." Annie's family, and more families and friends, huddled in their stone cellar "low enough to escape the cannon balls and the shells" and strong enough to protect "against the musket or rifle balls of the sharpshooters."

Not everyone escaped unscathed. A shell struck the house of Thomas Jenkins, shattering it badly and injuring his family. An unknown woman was killed on High Street. An African American woman who had ventured forth for water was also killed, her lifeless body stranded on Shenandoah Street all day. A shell penetrated the house of James McGraw on High Street, but passed directly through without injuring anyone. Its momentum carried it into an adjoining house "where it fell on a bed without exploding." Miss Margaret Kelly was in the room "when the unwelcome visitor intruded and settled down on the bed." Even Annie Marmion's refuge was no longer safe. A shell crashed through a dormer window, startling the refugees and "covering them with plaster and broken slate." Another dropped "in their very midst, but fortunately into the unsightly hogshead of water where it boils and hisses, steams and sputters," but does not explode. Neighbor Joseph Barry, who had escaped from the Ferry and now watched the bombardment from Maryland Heights, "remonstrated in strong language with the gunners for doing wanton mischief to inoffensive citizens."

General Sigel was more concerned about the Maryland side of the river. Throughout the day on July 6, Confederates probed all along his Maryland Heights defenses, searching for a weakness. The enemy line

Dr. Nicholas Marmion and his family resided in Harpers Ferry throughout the war despite persecution for his pro-Southern leanings. Dr. Marmion helped care for Confederate and civilian wounded during the 1864 bombardment of Harpers Ferry. (HFNHP)

Opposite page, top: *Bolivar and Bolivar Heights shortly after the war, as viewed from Camp Hill. General Early's Confederates pushed across the naked heights into the town, making it an inviting target for Union cannoneers on Maryland Heights.* (HFNHP)

Opposite page, bottom: *Signalmen on Maryland Heights communicated reports of the Confederate invasion to Sugarloaf Mountain, 30 miles southeast of Harpers Ferry. From there, flagmen waved their coded signals to a receiving station in Washington, D.C.* (LOC, Sketch by A. R. Waud)

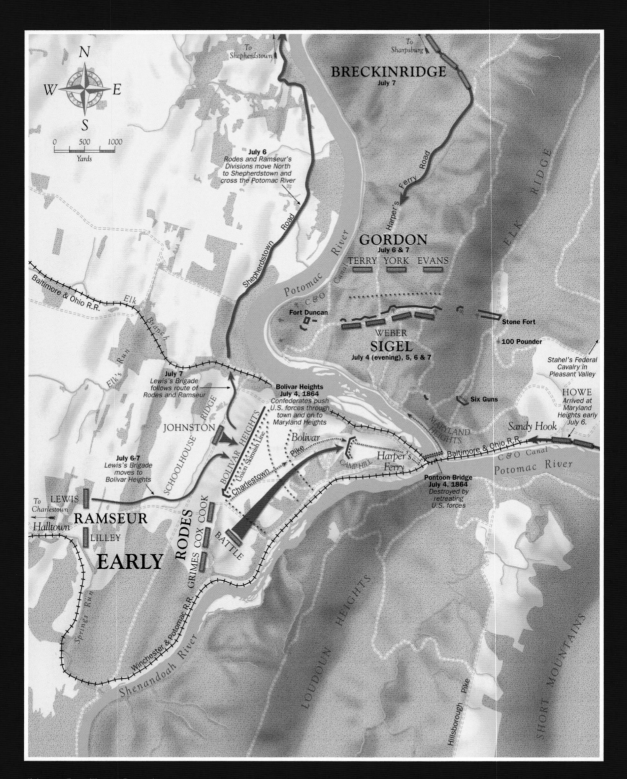

(Map by Gene Thorp © 2000)

extended nearly two miles from the Potomac to the top of Elk Ridge. The Confederates tested Sigel's left along the river and near Fort Duncan, but they failed to turn the flank. The next day, the Confederates advanced to within 600 yards of the Union defenses. "The enemy made preparation for a general attack," reported Sigel. The guns on Maryland Heights opened fire. The Confederates tried to bring artillery into position to support the attack, but were "unable to do so on account of the field batteries and heavy [cannon] pieces in the forts, which shelled their artillery, infantry, and trains for a distance of four miles."

A frustrated Jubal Early did not expect the Maryland Heights defenders to remain. They had evacuated the mountain during Stonewall's siege in 1862 and again during the Gettysburg Campaign in 1863. Early anticipated their departure once again. "Old Jube" had expended four days about Harpers Ferry, trying to remove the Yankees. They would not oblige this time. "My desire had been to maneuver the enemy out of Maryland Heights," Early revealed, "But he had taken refuge in his strongly fortified works, and as they could not be approached without great difficulty. . . . I determined to move [around] the heights."

This 100-pounder Parrott Rifle cannon could hurl a 100-pound projectile more than two miles with deadly accuracy. It set atop Maryland Heights and could be rotated 360 degrees, enabling Union cannoneers to attack Confederates approaching from any direction. The gun's very presence on top of the mountain was an engineering feat, considering the cannon tube alone weighed nearly five tons. (NPS/HFCCAC/ Hugh Brown)

Confederates sought shelter in houses along High Street during the bombardment from Maryland Heights. This photograph, taken in the postwar period, shows the buildings little changed since 1864. (HFNHP)

> *"If the war is to last another year, we want the Shenandoah Valley to remain a barren waste."*
>
> —**General Ulysses S. Grant**

"No signs of the enemy could be seen on our front," the signal station reported on the morning of July 8. General Early's army had rushed east toward Frederick, interposed between Maryland Heights and Washington, and General Sigel was cut off from the capital. The danger had passed for Harpers Ferry, however. Now all eyes focused on Washington. The defenders of Maryland Heights had stalled Early for four days—four days that earned General Grant invaluable time to rush troops into the empty defenses of Washington. The Confederates slowed for a day near Frederick, where they pushed aside a pieced-together Federal force in the Battle of Monocacy. Early's army then came within a few miles of the White House before their advance was halted at the Battle of Fort Stevens. Maryland Heights had met its final test of the Civil War. Never again did the Confederates threaten the "citadel of Harpers Ferry."

Saturday, July 9, 1864, marked a milestone in Harpers Ferry's Civil War history—the town changed hands for the final time. North and South had swapped possession of the Ferry eight times in three years. When the Federals rowed across the river to reoccupy the town on July 9, they stayed for the remainder of the war. Joseph Barry later reflected, "Although peace was not restored to the whole country for many months after this, Harper's Ferry was happily exempted from any more of its accustomed calamitous evacuations."

Sheridan's Campaign

*E*verywhere Charles Moulton looked he saw destruction. "The Quartermaster's storehouse was all in flames, the Gov't bakery had been totally destroyed and the R.R. platform was in ruins." Moulton passed 20,000 bushels of oats and corn in a smoldering "mass of coals." The "Johnny's" had gone into the saloons and "after drinking all they could, turned the spigots on and let the contents of the barrels run on the floor." In one store two barrels of coal oil had been ruptured, covering the floor with odorous and flammable fluid about one inch deep. Houses were destroyed, including one occupied by a widow "who lost everything. . . . It was a pitiful sight to see her and her aged mother and three little children; all they possessed in the world was what they wore on their backs." In Moulton's provost marshal office on High Street, six bullets had penetrated the building. He concluded the Confederates "visited every building and did all the damage they had time for."

Following the scare on Washington, General Early returned to the Shenandoah Valley and planted his

Sheridan's headquarters in the former armory paymaster's house. Newspaper artist James E. Taylor's rendering was such an accurate and detailed depiction that National Park Service architects used it to guide the building's exterior restoration 100 years after the war. (FRANK LESLIE'S ILLUSTRATED NEWSPAPER)

army firmly along the Potomac border. The distraction had worked—General Grant had been forced to siphon troops away from beleaguered Richmond and Petersburg. Early's new mission was to continue the distraction and aggressively act as a menacing threat. He responded with alacrity. He disrupted the B&O Railroad, destroying tracks and bridges without impediment. The Harpers Ferry bridge was rebuilt and opened 16 days following its destruction, but it mattered little as the trains could not safely pass further west. Early's cavalry ransomed the cities of Hagerstown and Frederick, threatening fiery destruction if the bankers did not pay the bounty. When its citizens failed to honor a ransom, Chambersburg, Pennsylvania, did go up in flames—the only Northern city destroyed during the war. Early's strategy of harassment, intimidation, and irritation prompted a Federal response. "We have 7 Generals here now," Charles Moulton wrote. "I think we will have a regiment of them here soon."

More than a regiment arrived. U. S. Grant sent an entire Union army.

General Grant issued adamant instructions for a fresh Shenandoah strategy. "Give the enemy no rest," he ordered Major General Philip H. Sheridan, his hand-selected new commander for the Shenandoah Valley army. "Follow him to the death." Wipe out General Early, but also make war on the population. "Do all the damage to railroads and crops you can. Carry off stock of all

Before arriving, Major General Philip H. Sheridan had met with President Lincoln in Washington. The President commented, after assessing Sheridan's odd proportions, that he was "the only man he ever met who could scratch his ankles without stooping." (NARA)

descriptions, and negroes, so as to prevent further planting." Grant intended to end this war through the dual punch of defeating the Confederate army and breaking the will of the Southern people.

Phil Sheridan had a reputation. The West Point graduate had served under Grant as an infantry commander, and recently had led Grant's cavalry operating against General Lee. Sheridan was aggressive in combat, progressive in strategy, and impressive in results. No previous Federal commander in the Shenandoah—

Brigadier General George Armstrong Custer commanded Union cavalry units during Sheridan's Shenandoah Valley Campaign. Here Custer begins his crusade in the Valley, arriving at Harpers Ferry and passing by John Brown's Fort. (WESTERN RESERVE HISTORICAL SOCIETY)

the "Valley of Death" for Union generals—had defeated the Confederates here. Grant had confidence that Sheridan would break that record.

General Sheridan arrived at Harpers Ferry on August 6, and promptly established his headquarters at the Lockwood House. James E. Taylor, a sketch artist assigned to cover Sheridan's army for *Frank Leslie's Illustrated Newspaper*, found Sheridan an interesting specimen. "His head was abnormally large with projecting bumps which from a phrenologist's view denoted combativeness. His body and arms were long while his pedals were disproportionately short, 'duck legs,' in fact." Taylor, who met Sheridan for the first time at the Lockwood House to request a horse, further noted, "The general's voice was anything but musical and when exercised under excitement, had a rasping sound, and croaking intonation when in its normal key."

Sheridan identified Harpers Ferry as his base of operations. His army was almost triple the size of the Valley's previous Federal armies. Nearly 50,000 infantrymen, cavalrymen, and artillerymen depended on quartermaster, commissary, and ordnance supplies from the Ferry. Soon the depot buzzed with so much activity that "there was nothing but a perfect jam all day and night in the streets," recorded Corporal Moulton. Fortifications were strengthened across Bolivar Heights. Enclosed behind the ridge was the largest mule corral and wagon park in the Shenandoah Valley. Thousands of mules and hundreds of white-canvassed wagons rotated to and from the corral as the Federal army commenced its supply shuttle service.

Hundreds of civilians were hired by the government to support this massive logistics operation. Storekeepers, and storehouse and receiving clerks,

Tons of army supplies were stored in the old armory buildings. (LOC, Sketch by A. R. Waud)

The odor of fresh-baked bread filled the Harpers Ferry air during the months of Sheridan's Shenandoah Valley Campaign. (LOC, Sketch by A. R. Waud)

tracked tons of quartermaster goods. Forage masters watched over oats and hay for the mule teams. A veterinary surgeon cared for the creatures while masters of transportation and the superintendent of the corral coordinated the mule labor. Blacksmiths, wheelwrights, carpenters, saddlers, and painters maintained the wagons. The wagon master supervised the trains and the teamsters drove the mules. And dozens of laborers loaded and stacked the wares. The rolls showed 289 civilians performing 35 different jobs. Not since the days of the armory had so many civilians been on the government payroll.

And pay was good. Joseph Barry worked as the forage master at a salary of $75 per month—almost five times the pay of a private. The superintendent of the corral, veterinary surgeon, boss wheelwright, boss carpenter, brigade wagon master, and the superintendent of laborers drew equal amounts as Barry. Only the storekeeper, master of transportation, and the master mechanic received more ($100 per month).

The pay was exceptional but not always guaranteed. Captain George A. Flagg, the quartermaster at Harpers Ferry, became "much embarrassed to procure the requisite labor required in his department because of his inability to pay the Government employees." Flagg had been operating the post for several months, but during that time had been "compelled to run his Department without a dollar." He pleaded with the War Department: "Many of the Quarter Master employees are poor men, relying upon their daily labor to support themselves and families, and are literally without money." Flagg's superior

Running Number	No. of each Class	NAMES OF PERSONS AND ARTICLES.	DESIGNATION AND OCCUPATION.	SERVICE DURING THE MONTH.			RATE OF HIRE OR COMPENSATION.			DATE OF	BY WHOM OWNED.
				From	To	Days.	Dollars.	Cents.	Days, month, or voyage.		
		Stephen Conley	Labour in	23	30	8	20	00	mo.	Sep 23 64	
		Henry Brucher	Forage House	26	30	5	30	00	"	" 26 "	
		Hw Brucher	"	29	30	2	30	00	"	" 29 "	
		Saughlin Sloan	"	23	30	8	30	00	"	" 23 "	
		John Dailey	"	22	30	9	30	00	"	" 22 "	
		Joseph Wyman	"	10	30	21	30	00	"	Sep 10 "	
		Lewis Neh	"	29	30	2	30	00	"	" 29 "	
		Sidney Freeman	"	27	30	4	30	00	"	" 27 "	
		Jacob Sehn	"	10	30	21	30	00	"	" 10 "	
		John H Boon	"	10	22	13	30	00			
		Lewis B Boots	"	10	23	14	30	00			
		Goram Moseley	"	10	23	14	30	00			
		Ezra Conrad	"	10	23	14	30	00			
		R Sailer	"	10	23	14	30	00			
		Harry Hunter	"	1	24	24	30	00			
		Chas H Houck	"	13	30	18	30	00		13	
		John Gray	"	1	30	30	30	00		1	
		John Halpin	"	1	30	30	30	00		1	
		Thos Slavin	"	1	30	30	30	00		1	
		John Beckam	"	15	17	3	30	00		15	
		Jacob M Shoemaker	"	19	23	5	30	00		19	
		Austin Runner	"	10	30	21	30	00		10	
		Clarence Newport	"	10	22	13	30	00		10	
		Arch Waters	"	1	30	30	30	00		1	
		Sampson Sines	"	1	30	30	30	00		1	
		Hugh Smith	"	1	30	30	30	00		1	
		Tood Johnson	"	13	30	18	30	00		13	
		John Wesley	"	7	30	24	25	00		7	
		John Smith	"	1	30	30	30	00		1	
		Thomas Jackson	"	10	30	21	30	00		10	
		John Isaac	"	10	30	21	30	00		10	
		Jacob Lappsetz	"	10	30	21	25	00		10	
		F R Walter	"	10	30	21	30	00		10	
		James Weak	"	12	30	19	30	00		12	
		Saml Mitchell	"	10	16	7	30	00		10	
		Geo M Schill	"	10	16	7	30	00		10	
		John Weaver	"	10	30	21	30	00		10	
		G F Goodman	"	10	16	7	30	00		10	
		John Young	"	10	15	6	30	00		10	

Amount of rent and hire during the month..............

I CERTIFY, ON HONOR, that the above is a true copy of all the persons and articles employed and hired by me during the

Entries in the quartermaster's accounting book. (HFNHP)

officer labeled this practice "a great injustice to the laborer," and believed it brought the government disrespect. The plea ended with a warning: "The present demand for every soldier in the field is ample reason why such a condition should not exist. Otherwise, enlisted men will be drawn upon to perform all quarter master labor." This was the magic phrase. Pay arrived promptly.

Sheridan, a former quartermaster himself, understood that an army at the front could not fight and survive without logistics in the rear. "Little Phil" knew his success demanded a dependable, responsible, and tough manager who appreciated security and could deal with scrutiny. He selected a St. Louis lawyer and politician for the job. Brigadier General John Dunlop Stevenson arrived in mid-August. A native of the Valley of Virginia, Stevenson was a loyal Unionist. He had fought with Grant and Sheridan during their major campaigns in Tennessee, and now, at age 44, they called him "home" to clear the Rebels from his native Shenandoah Valley.

Stevenson established his headquarters at the master armorer's house, and took command over the newly designated Military District of Harpers Ferry. It consolidated, under one central command, various towns and depots along the B&O and W&P Railroads, along with adjoining counties. Stevenson had four missions: protect the railroads and depots; ensure safe transport, via wagon trains, to and from the front; meet and defeat Confederate guerillas; and enforce martial law. None of these were new to Harpers Ferry commanders, but they had all failed because they were never considered part of a singular, logistical mission. Stevenson summarized his purpose succinctly: "The loss of one train by a careless officer could defeat a campaign."

John Singleton Mosby considered enemy logistics his principal prey. "The line that connects an army with its base of supplies is the heel of

Brigadier General John Dunlop Stevenson (LOC)

The former residence of the master armorer (center left) on Shenandoah Street served as General Stevenson's headquarters. (WRHS)

Achilles—its most vital and vulnerable point," theorized Mosby. Colonel Mosby's "incessant attacks" were designed to compel the enemy either to "greatly contract his lines or to reinforce them." If he could draw Federal troops to the rear to protect lines, Sheridan would have fewer men to fight on the front, thus evening the odds for outnumbered Confederates. To carry out his strategy, Mosby identified three specific objectives: destroy supply trains; isolate an army from its base; and break up means of conveying intelligence.

Mosby struck first. The "Gray Ghost" spied a wagon train one week after Sheridan's arrival. The train totaled almost 1,000 wagons, stretching more than 10 miles, and requiring four hours to pass a single point. This was perfect fodder for Mosby. He ensnared his prey near Berryville, about 20 miles

south of the Ferry, where he burned wagons and departed with captured mules, cattle, and Federal prisoners. Following Berryville, however, not one successful Mosby interruption occurred in the Valley through the end of Sheridan's campaign in December. Despite ample opportunities, Mosby failed to disrupt wagon trains, interrupt essential railroad traffic, intercept Union reinforcements, or recover captured Confederates. Moreover, he failed in his overall mission to sever the enemy's supply lines. He failed because Sheridan and Stevenson introduced countermeasures that the guerilla chieftain could not overcome, such as aggressively chasing the guerillas and keeping them on the defensive.

A Federal cavalry patrol departs the Camp Hill fortifications in search of Confederate partisans (guerillas). This view shows the only opening in the fort at Washington Street. Cannon muzzles peek through the v-shaped "embrasures" within the earthworks. The house illustrated in the background still stands. (LOC, Sketch by A. R. Waud)

Mosby's attack on a supply train near Berryville, Virginia. (THE SOLDIER IN OUR CIVIL WAR)

Inset: *John Singleton Mosby, the Confederacy's most famous guerilla.* (LOC/PPOC)

Prisoners of War

Ascertaining that civilians harbored guerillas and provided them with intelligence, Stevenson crafted rules and regulations that restricted citizen movement, communication, and commerce. "The most stringent laws are now in force here," observed Charles Moulton. "All baggage belonging to civilians and all freight arriving [must be] searched to see that no smuggling is going on." No person living outside the limits of the district was allowed inside the lines, "except twice a month, and then his pass is limited to 6 hours each time." No person could procure more than $50 worth of supplies for an entire family per month. All goods required proper permits before they could pass through the lines.

Stevenson had an additional rule that made life even more uncomfortable. If any guerilla interruption occurred on the rebuilt Winchester and Potomac Railroad, "all disloyal residents of Charlestown, Shepherdstown, Berryville,

Both suppliers and buyers needed passes—approved by the provost marshal—before they could purchase food, supplies, and goods at the only permitted market in Harpers Ferry, located along the Shenandoah River. (WRHS)

and Smithfield are to be ousted and confined in Fort McHenry during the war and their house burned." General Sheridan had a warning for the residents astride the railroad in Jefferson County. "Those people who live in the vicinity of Harper's Ferry are the most villainous in this Valley, and have not yet been hurt much. If the railroad is interfered with, I will make some of them poor." Stevenson's General Orders No. 23 was posted every 300 feet along the entire 30-mile length of the W&P tracks. Not a single incident occurred.

While Stevenson conducted warfare behind the lines, Sheridan was busy smashing the Confederates up the Valley. Two days before "Little Phil" launched his campaign, General Grant traveled to Charles Town to confer with Sheridan via the B&O to Harpers Ferry. While at Harpers Ferry, Grant

spent the night of September 16 at General Stevenson's headquarters at the master armorer's house. "He is a very plain looking man," Charles Moulton described. "He always has a cigar in his mouth. He was here only two days and during that brief period used up a box of cigars."

In the next 32 days, Sheridan's men fought four major battles in the Valley—and won every one. The cannon on Maryland Heights fired 100-gun salutes to honor Sheridan's successes. Fifteen captured battle flags were paraded through Harpers Ferry by their proud captors. "The men who took the flags had the honor to convey them to Washington," admired Moulton, "where they were each the recipients of a handsome medal [the Medal of Honor]."

Thousands of captured Confederates were processed through Moulton's provost marshal office at Harpers Ferry. "I could not begin to tell you how busy we have been during the past few weeks," Moulton informed his mother at the end of the first week of October. "Altogether some 4,000 Rebels have passed through our hands." In just three weeks, Sheridan's battlefield successes had nabbed nearly one quarter of Early's army. Unlike 1862, when prisoners were paroled and exchanged, POWs were imprisoned in 1864.

The deluge of prisoners challenged General Stevenson. Transporting the captives from the front to the rear required armed escorts through miles of enemy territory. This presented an inviting target for Mosby. Yet Stevenson managed to match Mosby's wit, moving more than 7,000 Confederate prisoners to Harpers Ferry during Sheridan's Valley Campaign. Upon arrival, they were turned over to the provost marshal. Corporal Moulton, the most experienced clerk in the provost office, supervised the prisoner processing which involved four steps: identification, description, search, and shipment.

Lieutenant General Ulysses S. Grant (LOC)

High Street in 1864, rendered in architectural detail by Frank Leslie's Illustrated Newspaper *artist James E. Taylor. The provost office appears in the upper left of the drawing.* (WRHS)

Moulton was one of the first to witness and understand Sheridan's success. Before the end of August—prior to any major engagement—Moulton's workload dramatically increased. "Since Sheridan's operations commenced we have had an average of about 100 prisoners every day. . . . On one occasion a squad of 225 came in about 11 o'clock at night." These unprecedented numbers forced the provost marshal "to remove the Guard House to a large and more spacious building. It is now located in an old factory building, four stories high, the Federal, Rebel, and Citizen prisoners being placed in separate rooms." The building Moulton described was the former cotton mill on Virginius Island, previously used as a hospital. "The building being so high it requires a smaller guard than before, as the prisoners have no way to escape, but to leap out the windows and break their necks."

Even the new Guard House became inadequate as Moulton grappled with multiplying numbers. He counted 1,400 in one day alone. Soon, he learned that 2,000 more were coming from Martinsburg. "I wish I could have a chance to take a gaze at the pile of Rebs we have got 'corralled' in Bolivar tonight," Moulton addressed his brother. Before him in the lower town, he saw prisoners "stretched in line and [occupying] as much distance as from our house [on High Street] to the factory (nearly one-third mile).

It does seems as if we [will] never get through with them and it is a fixed certainty that we won't as long as 'Philly' travels about the Valley." Though amazed at the numbers, Moulton was more pleased with the Southerners' disposition. "A large number of them wish to take the oath [of allegiance to the United States]." Resigned Confederates rejoining the Union represented ultimate victory.

Before sending any prisoners forward, Moulton and his fellow clerks obtained names, ranks, and physical descriptions of each prisoner, including height, weight, eye and hair color, and complexion. Once identified, a prisoner was searched thoroughly. "You ought to see the pile of knives and other 'relics' we have on hand," Moulton described. After the officers were separated from the enlisted men, the prisoners were placed on guarded railroad cars for lengthy transports to prisons far away in Delaware, Maryland, New York, and Ohio.

George Q. Peyton of the 13th Virginia Infantry was one of the unfortunate Confederate prisoners who endured this process. Following his capture at the Battle of Cedar Creek on October 19, he arrived at Harpers Ferry three days later after being marched to Martinsburg and then trained to the Ferry. In darkness, Peyton was marched two miles to Bolivar Heights, where he had no fire, no water, and no food. The next day, suffering from hunger and thirst, he "bought a small apple pie for 10 cents in silver. The only piece I had. I do not know where I got it." Rations

Previously the "Island Hospital," the abandoned cotton mill (far left) on Virginius Island was transformed into a four-story prison during Sheridan's Shenandoah Valley Campaign. (HFNHP)

finally arrived, consisting of hard bread, bacon, mess pork, and soup. "They also brought us some wood and water," acknowledged Peyton, but it was "in pork barrels and not fit to drink and there was not enough to go around." After two nights on Bolivar Heights and one crowded night in an old armory building, Peyton was put on a train. Three days later, he arrived at a POW camp at Point Lookout, Maryland.

Women in Blue and Gray

"Among the Rebel prisoners lately brought in was a female Reb," Corporal Charles Moulton wrote to his brother. Sarah Mitchel, alias Charley West, had been serving with the 18th Virginia Cavalry. She was age 17, "with a delicate voice, and not very good looking." After escaping from the Guard House at the Ferry, Moulton defined her as "a spunky little specimen of the feminine gender." After her recapture, she boasted she would escape again, but she was whisked away to Washington instead. Another female found in uniform was Maggie Simpson. "She was a rather scaly looking specimen of the human frame, has a face similar to a crocodile and a voice as sweet as a cracked fiddle or an old cow bell or bellows!" Simpson was rushed away for imprisonment at Fort McHenry in Baltimore.

Occasionally the Harpers Ferry provost office encountered women wearing Union blue. One, whose voice betrayed her as a "false man," belonged to the 19th Corps in Sheridan's army. She said she had adopted the attire "for the good of my country." She was arrested and sent home to Pennsylvania. Another female soldier claimed she had joined the ranks to accompany her "'fond lover' through the various vicissitudes of life, war, etc." Moulton enjoyed her spunk. "She goes in decidedly for 'woman's rights' and has been placed in confinement for insulting the General Commanding. While before him she too freely expressed her opinions and bragged about her independent qualities and no 'shoulder strap' should order her and similar language."

Moulton's favorite female soldier story involved two women riding with the 1st West Virginia Cavalry. They had served with the regiment for 10 months, "making very good looking boys." But they were discovered during a surgeon's examination. "They were tanned and sunburnt all well enough, but their voice betrayed them. . . . Not many would have denied but that they were really boys, they were so perfectly 'initiated.'"

Sarah Emma Edmonds joined the 2nd Michigan Volunteer Infantry disguised as Private Franklin Thompson. She served as a male nurse, spy, and solider for the war's first two years, until illness forced her to desert from the army to prevent exposing her true identity. She arrived at Harpers Ferry during the final year of the war as a female nurse. (Courtesy Archives of Michigan)

The Fourth Winter of the War

*N*ovember 1864 brought another lull to the Valley. Sheridan had conquered Early, the Mosby menace had subsided, and the Union army had completed its task of leaving the Valley barren. No surrender had occurred, however, so Sheridan's men prepared to go into winter quarters.

The Winchester and Potomac Railroad, completely rebuilt to handle larger engines and longer trains, became the army's main line of supply, ultimately employing 13 engines, 75 cars, and nearly 600 men in its operation. The military transformed the old Rifle Factory Island (Hall's lower island) into Sheridan's depot. An engine house and machine shop were constructed

to maintain the rolling stock, and extensive platforms were erected for the loading of quartermaster and commissary stores for shipment. During the final months of the war, 2,238 trains passed over the W&P, transporting nearly 200,000 people.

With the Shenandoah Valley secured, General Grant needed Sheridan's troops to help break the Confederate defenses around Richmond and Petersburg and force the collapse of the Confederacy. On December 1, Sheridan began transporting thousands of bluecoats out of the Valley. With most of the army gone, Harpers Ferry quieted considerably. It was the fourth winter of the war. Sheridan's departure brought hope to Charles Moulton. "Next year at this time I will be pursuing the peaceful avocation of civil life once more."

Troop transports on the Winchester and Potomac (W&P) Railroad are visible in this view from Jefferson Rock at the end of Sheridan's Shenandoah Valley Campaign. Ruins of the bridge across the Shenandoah appear in the background, and a pontoon bridge is present at far right. The steeple at left center denotes a church along Shenandoah Street. Not a single building in the photograph survives today. (U.S. Military Academy)

The 5th New York Heavy Artillery remained at Harpers Ferry during the war's last winter to man the cannon on Maryland Heights in case of a Confederate incursion. None occurred. This regulation camp on a gentle slope before the former armory superintendent's quarters is laid out in precise company streets, and each company has its own kitchen and mess hall (row of buildings at base of camp). The Camp Hill fortification (top) forms the camp's western perimeter. (HFNHP, DRAWING BY WARD S. DAY, 5TH NEW YORK, COMPANY C, LITHOGRAPH BY E. SACHS AND COMPANY)

CAMP HILL, HARPER'S FERRY, VA

A Most Sickening Affair

William Loge, known also as "French Bill," was notorious as a guerilla bushwhacker, murderer, and assassin. A deserter from a Union regiment prior to joining the Confederate cause, "French Bill" epitomized the worst criminal of war for Federal authorities. The day following his capture, he was fated for execution.

"An immense crowd assembled on the ground [of Bolivar Heights] and the procession arrived about 3:00 p.m.—headed by the Post Band," Charles Moulton recorded. Harpers Ferry resident Joseph Barry attended, noting morosely "there [was] no phase of war that was not experienced at some time by its people." Moulton listened as the criminal admitted his crimes from the scaffold, including desertion and attacking Yankee soldiers, and expressed his only wish was "to see his mother." In a moment the hatchet sprang; the trap door dropped. As the prisoner dangled, the rope snapped. "The poor prisoner in his last struggles of agony, while being brought to the scaffolding a second time, cried that they would only shoot him and put him out of his misery."

Moulton declared he "never wanted to witness another execution of this kind." Joseph Barry concurred. "On the whole it was the most sickening affair witnessed at the place during the war."

Corporal Moulton had part of his wish granted. The next execution was by firing squad rather than a hanging. Deserter Thomas Murphy, alias Patrick Powers of the 6th U.S. Cavalry, had changed his name and jumped from regiment to regiment to collect enlistment bonuses. Known as "bounty jumping," this was the most despicable crime for the soldier in the ranks. "Bounty jumping" was intolerable, and General Sheridan ordered the man executed following his court martial trial.

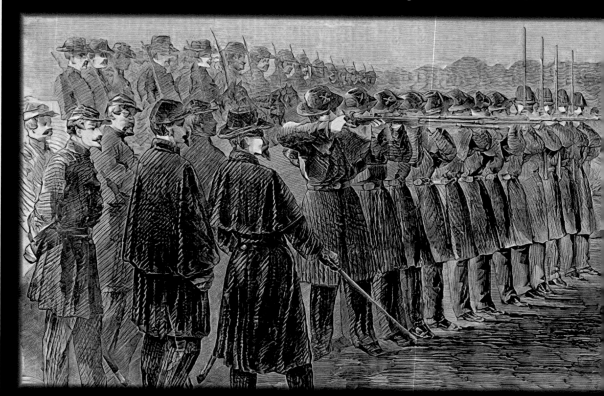

The execution again occurred on Bolivar Heights. Two bands led the procession with the Death March. A square of soldiers surrounded the condemned man, who was placed on his coffin. A chaplain administered the last rights of the Catholic faith, then Murphy spoke, stating he was innocent and that he had been tried by a prejudiced court. Corporal Moulton had "the disagreeable task of tieing [sic] his hands and placing a bandage around his eyes." Then the command "Fire!" and six bullets pierced his chest. Charles Moulton wanted nothing more to do with this part of the war. "I have now seen both a hanging and a shooting execution and they are enough for me."

SPECIAL ORDERS,
No. 176.

WAR DEPARTMENT,
ADJUTANT GENERAL'S OFFICE,
Washington, April 18th, 1865.

(*Extract.*)

*   *   *   *   *

2. Private *James Brown*, a recruit of the 6th U. S. Cavalry, now under sentence of death at Harper's Ferry, Virginia, is pardoned, and will be returned to duty with that regiment.

The Quartermaster's Department will furnish the necessary transportation

*   *   *   *   *

By order of the President of the United States :

E. D. TOWNSEND,
Assistant Adjutant General.

The President often pardoned convicted soldiers. This one occurred nine days after Lee's surrender. (HFNHP)

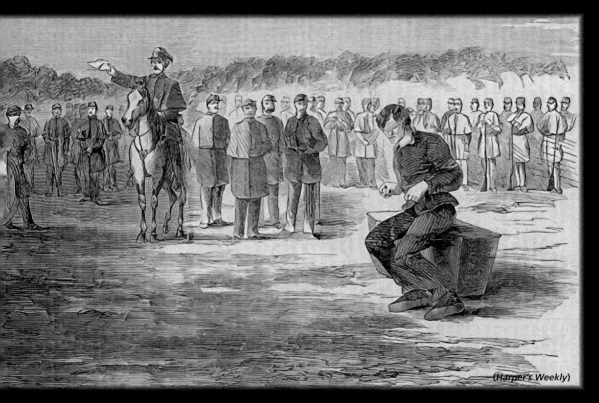

(*Harper's Weekly*)

"Sweet Johnny"

Born and raised near Harpers Ferry, on the opposite bank of the Shenandoah in Loudoun County, John Mobberly organized "a reckless band of cut throats and marauders, robbing every soldier they came across, stealing horses from the citizens and committing all sorts of daring dep-redations." Among his ignominious crimes was the barbaric murder of a Harpers Ferry schoolmaster named Law. The teacher from New York aggressively advocated abolition, so much that he was driven out of town after the John Brown affair for expressing his sentiments strongly. During the war, Mobberly's gang snatched Mr. Law and determined to make him an example. They carried their prisoner to Loudoun Heights and staked him to the ground. "There he was left to perish of hunger, thirst, cold, or any more speedy death from the fangs of wild animals."

John Mobberly (HFNHP)

Mobberly continued terrorizing the region until April 5, 1865, four days before the surrender of General Lee. Residents in Loudoun County conspired with Union cavalry to set an ambush for Mobberly. The trap worked. A detachment of four Loudoun Rangers assassinated the unsus-pecting gangster. "His body, with the head perforated in three places by bullets, was thrown, like a sack of grain, across [his] horse's back and conveyed in triumph to Harper's Ferry where it was exposed to public view in front of headquarters," recounted resi-dent Joseph Barry. Corporal Charles Moulton remembered the spectacle of Mobberly's corpse. "A large crowd assembled around his body. He was an awful looking sight, covered with blood from head to foot and his hands were completely dyed in blood which were caused to be clutch-ing at his wounds in agony."

Joseph Barry watched as "the body was almost denuded by relic hunters who, with their jack knives, cut pieces off his clothes as souvenirs of the war." Moulton expressed relief. "His career has come to a sudden end and the community is ridden of its greatest terror."

Fifteen months after Moulton's regiment first arrived in Harpers Ferry, the war had reduced its numbers from more than 600 to 66. The 34th Massachusetts lost its regimental colonel, major, and many comrades. Death after death had separated Moulton and countless others from the sensibilities of life. When two bodies washed up against the Potomac shore, names unknown and from unknown places, little attention was paid. "No inquests were held over these mysterious bodies, but they were merely thrown into a grave and will soon be forgotten. . . . How changed are matters," Moulton wrote. "In civil times, what a stir was created if a man or any person was found dead. But in war times a person's life is worth merely nothing."

The Return of Peace

"Affairs begin to look bright on the war horizon," Charles Moulton eagerly announced to his mother as spring arrived in Harpers Ferry in 1865. "Everyone seems to feel enlivened over the glorious news constantly received from day to day."

Further south in Virginia, the combined forces of Grant and Sheridan proved too much for General Lee. The Confederates evacuated Richmond and Petersburg. When the grand news reached Harpers Ferry, orders went to the batteries on Maryland Heights to fire a 100-gun salute. The honor commenced at 6:00 a.m. Cannon thundered every 30 seconds until 100 salutes had occurred. One week later, on Palm Sunday, April 9, 1865, Robert E. Lee surrendered the Army of Northern Virginia. The Maryland Heights cannon erupted again. The celebration was short-lived, however. President Lincoln was assassinated on April 15. In a salute for the late president, 20 guns per minute fired during the noon hour. From sunrise to sunset, a single gun fired every 30 minutes in honor of Lincoln's memory. As the cannon exploded, one could recall the flames from the Harpers Ferry arsenal that had illuminated the night sky almost exactly four years earlier. What had four years wrought?

SURRENDER OF GEN! LEE, AT APPOMATTOX C. H. V.ª APRIL 9TH 1865.

(LOC/PPOC)

Epilogue

"It may be said with truth that no place in the United States experienced more of the horrors of war," wrote Joseph Barry. "The first act of the great tragedy—the Brown raid—was enacted there, and at no time until the curtain fell, was Harper's Ferry entirely unconnected with the performance."

Still young in age, Annie Marmion had matured with the experiences of four years of war. "What a God forsaken place! Is the exclamation of many who see this War scarred Hamlet." She was amazed when 500 bullets were pulled from a neighbor's roof.

Dunn Browne spoke best for the soldiers of both sides. Thirty months before the war ended he foreshadowed: "I assure you that our soldiers will be the ones of all others to rejoice with joy unspeakable over the return of peace. War—certainly as conducted on the principles of the present one—proves its own best antidote. The man who has seen its horrid face fears it most. There is only one thing that is worse, and that is our country destroyed, our liberties lost, and our precious institutions perished."

With the ratification of the Thirteenth Amendment, slavery was one of the institutions that perished. After the war, Harpers Ferry became a headquarters of the Freedmen's Bureau. Men and women previously bonded by slavery now had to construct new lives. They had an advocate in Reverend Nathan G. Brackett, who arrived from Maine with a mission to educate the newly freed people of color. Brackett believed in a hopeful future as he started his school at the Lockwood House, a building with past ties to slavery. A former paymaster

Waterwheels that once powered the machinery of the armory rusted and rotted in the decades following the Civil War. The town—crippled by war and repeated flooding—struggled to avoid similar decay. (HFNHP)

Reverend Nathan G. Brackett
(HFNHP)

who lived there was a slave owner. Contraband slaves helped operate the hospital there. And slaves were sheltered in the house during Jackson's siege and roundup. Now former slaves came here to be educated and assume their new role as citizens. Brackett and his students inspired philanthropist John Storer of Sanford, Maine, to donate $10,000 for the establishment of a school in the South that would not discriminate against sex, race, or religion. On October 2, 1867, on the denuded area of Camp Hill, in former armory buildings once occupied by the military, "Storer Normal School" (later Storer College) was opened.

Reverend Brackett no doubt smiled at the prospect, but shuddered at the reality. "Before the war Harper's Ferry lived on the Armory; during the war on the Army. Whether it lives at all in the future depends on the action of the Government. Perhaps this town suffered more by war, and more by its close than any other town."

Some citizens did return to Harpers Ferry, only to find their homes occupied or destroyed. Efforts to reestablish business and industry were repeatedly dashed by Shenandoah and Potomac River floods. The town nearly perished. But the memory of John Brown's attempt to deliver slaves to their freedom continued to draw visitors. In August 1906, the Niagara Movement (later the NAACP) held its first public meeting in the United States on the campus of Storer College. Nearly 80 years after the Civil War, Reverend Brackett's desire for the "action of the Government" finally came to fruition when the U.S.

Tent shelters, pictured here after the war at the armory entrance, offered African Americans temporary homes as they commenced the transition from slavery to freedom. The former residence of the master armorer (center background) became the headquarters for the Freedmen's Bureau serving the district surrounding Harpers Ferry.
(NARA)

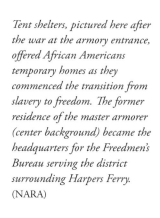

Congress established the Harpers Ferry National Monument (later changed to Historical Park).

Through decades of research, interpretation, archeology, and preservation, the National Park Service has been able to share the significant story of Harpers Ferry in the Civil War. Where the two rivers converge and the majestic heights soar, much of the Lower Town's prewar appearance has been restored, and its streets are now protected as an historical landmark. The dedicated efforts of historians, rangers, and volunteers continue today, ensuring that the stories of the soldiers who fought here and the citizens who lived and died here will not be forgotten.

Top: *Commerce returned to Harpers Ferry following the war, as evidenced by the merchant advertising on High Street. Civilians no longer required passes or permission from the provost office (far right) to conduct business. Nor did people have to fear bullets or shells when walking up the Stone Steps (far left). Without the armory or another major industry to replace it, Harpers Ferry never regained its antebellum bustle or prosperity.* (HFNHP)

Bottom: *The famous structure as it appeared nearly 30 years after John Brown's Raid—a survivor of war, and a symbol of freedom.* (LOC, Thomas Featherstonhaugh Collection)

Surplus army tents provided homes for former slaves concentrated at Harpers Ferry, where they received assistance from the newly established U.S. Freedmen's Bureau in the months following the war. Refugees obtained food, temporary shelter, and some education as they sought jobs and new homes as free people. (LOC)

Harpers Ferry in the early 21st century. (NPS, HFC)

Harpers Ferry Civil War Chronology

1859

October 16–18 John Brown's Raid on the U.S. Armory and Arsenal.

November 2 John Brown sentenced to hang.

December 2 John Brown executed in Charles Town, Virginia.

1860

November 6 Abraham Lincoln elected the 16th president.

December 20 South Carolina secedes.

1861

April 12–14 Fort Sumter in Charleston, South Carolina, is fired upon by Confederate troops.

April 15 President Lincoln calls for 75,000 volunteers to suppress rebellion and form a Union army.

April 17 Virginia secedes.

April 18 Federal troops set fire to the United States Armory and Arsenal.

April 19 2,400 Virginia volunteer militia occupy Harpers Ferry.

April 28 Colonel Thomas Jonathan Jackson takes command of Virginia volunteers at Harpers Ferry.

April–May Armory machinery and tools are shipped to Richmond, Virginia, and Fayetteville, North Carolina.

June 14–15 Confederate army evacuates Harpers Ferry; destroys U.S. Armory and B&O Railroad bridge.

June 28 Confederates return and burn the U.S. Rifle Factory on Hall's Island and the Shenandoah bridge.

July 4 Frederick Roeder is the first civilian killed during the war.

July 25 Approximately 7,000 Federal troops occupy Harpers Ferry.

August 17 Federals withdraw to Maryland shore.

October 16 Battle of Bolivar Heights.

October 18 Confederate forces burn Herr's flour mill.

1862

February 7 Federal soldiers burn the commercial area near "The Point."

February 25 Federals occupy the town to maintain

John Brown's men defend their "Fort." (HFNHP)

Confederates abandon Harpers Ferry and destroy B&O Railroad bridge and cars.
(*HARPER'S WEEKLY*)

communication and supply lines along the B&O Railroad and launch first invasion of the Shenandoah Valley.

February 26 Federal troops complete a pontoon bridge across the Potomac River.

May–June Stonewall Jackson's Shenandoah Valley Campaign.

May Union Army and U.S. Navy construct a naval artillery battery on Maryland Heights.

May 29–30 General Stonewall Jackson probes the defenses of Federal positions on Bolivar Heights.

September 4 General Robert E. Lee begins first invasion of the North.

September 9 Lee issues Special Orders No. 191, sending three columns to capture or destroy the Federal garrison at Harpers Ferry.

September 13–15 Battle of Harpers Ferry.

September 15 Approximately 12,700 Federal soldiers surrender to Stonewall Jackson at Harpers Ferry.

September 17 Battle of Antietam.

September 18 Confederates evacuate Harpers Ferry.

September 20 Federals occupy Harpers Ferry and soon begin extensive fortifications on the Heights.

October 1–2 President Lincoln reviews Federal troops at Harpers Ferry.

1863

January 1 President Lincoln issues the Emancipation Proclamation.

April–May U.S. Army Engineer, General John Barnard, plans and recommends extensive fortifications in and around Harpers Ferry.

(NPS)

June Federal troops add 100-pounder artillery piece and a series of breastworks on Maryland Heights.

A 100-pounder Parrott shot case shell, similar to the type fired from Maryland Heights. (NPS/DIP)

June 16 General Robert E. Lee begins second invasion of the North.

June 17 Federal troops evacuate Harpers Ferry and man fortifications on Maryland Heights.

June 20 West Virginia admitted to the Union as the 35th state.

June 30 Federals abandon Maryland Heights; withdraw to Frederick, Maryland.

June 30 12th Virginia Cavalry attacks Union cavalry on Bolivar Heights, capturing Federal soldiers and occupying Harpers Ferry.

July 1–3 Battle of Gettysburg.

July 7 Federal troops reoccupy Maryland Heights.

July 14 Federal troops reoccupy Harpers Ferry and reconstruct Potomac pontoon bridge.

1864

January 10 Colonel John S. Mosby's Partisan Rangers suffer a rare defeat following their failed ambush of Union Major

Henry Cole's Maryland Cavalry on Loudoun Heights.

March 19 U.S. Colored Troops march through Harpers Ferry.

July 4 General Jubal Early forces Union soldiers to withdraw to Maryland Heights. Bombardment by Federal troops forces Early back and delays attack on Washington.

July 7 Federal forces reoccupy Harpers Ferry. The town changes hands for the last time.

August–October Sheridan's Shenandoah Valley Campaign.

August–December Union General Philip Sheridan establishes base of operations at Harpers Ferry. Soldiers construct earthwork defenses

along the crest of Bolivar Heights.

September 16–17 Union General Ulysses S. Grant convenes council of war with Sheridan and stays overnight in Harpers Ferry.

November 8 President Lincoln reelected.

1865

March 3 Freedmen's Bureau established.

April 2 Richmond, Virginia, capital of the Confederacy, falls.

April 5 Confederate guerrilla and Harpers Ferry native John Mobberly is shot and killed by Federal cavalry near Lovettsville, Virginia.

April 9 General Robert E. Lee surrenders to General Ulysses S. Grant at Appomattox Courthouse.

April 14 President Lincoln assassinated.

June 30 Federal troops at Harpers Ferry are mustered out of service.

The ruins of the smith and forging shop—once the pride of the U.S. Armory and the depot for the U.S. Army—stood as a witness to Harpers Ferry's turbulent past. (HFNHP)

Union supply train departing through the defenses of Camp Hill during Sheridan's 1864 Shenandoah Valley Campaign. (WRHS)

Selected and Annotated Bibliography

1861

Barry, Joseph. *The Strange Story of Harper's Ferry*. Martinsburg, West Virginia: Thompson Brothers, 1903. Firsthand account of the outbreak of war, the early occupations, and the first year of destruction and abandonment.

Frye, Dennis E. "Stonewall's Dilemma: Guns and Politics at Harpers Ferry." *America's Civil War*. Vol. 24, No. 2, May 2011. A concise history of Thomas Jonathan Jackson's first command of the war and his incursion into Maryland territory and Confederate politics.

Geary, John W. "Skirmish at Bolivar Heights, Report." *The War of the Rebellion: A Compilation of the Official Records of the Union and Confederate Armies*. Vol. 5, Series 1. Washington: Government Printing Office, United States War Department, 1902. Detailed Union account of the first engagement at Harpers Ferry.

Gordon, George H. *Brook Farm to Cedar Mountain in the War of the Great Rebellion, 1861–1862*. Boston: James R. Osgood and Company, 1883. Fine description of the first U.S. occupation of Harpers Ferry and the Shenandoah Valley by the commander of the 2nd Massachusetts Infantry.

Imboden, John D. "Jackson at Harper's Ferry in 1861." *Battles and Leaders of the Civil War*. Vol. 1. New York: The Century Company, 1887. Reminiscence of the early Southern occupation.

Strother, David Hunter. "Personal Recollections of the War, by a Virginian." *Harper's New Monthly Magazine*. Vol. 1. New York: 1861–1862. Eyewitness account of the burning of the arsenal and the early months of the war.

Quint, Alonzo H. *The Record of the Second Massachusetts Infantry*. Boston: James P. Walker, 1867. Reflections of the chaplain of the first U.S. regiment to enter Harpers Ferry following Confederate abandonment.

Stearns, Austin C. *Three Years in Company K.* Cranbury, New Jersey: Associated University Presses, Inc., 1976. Account of the 13th Massachusetts Infantry guarding the Potomac River border during the summer and early fall.

1862

Bauer, K. Jack, ed. *Soldiering: The Civil War Diary of Rice C. Bull*. San Rafael, California: Presidio Press, 1977. Best soldier description of conditions at the Island Hospital, along with details on 123rd New York encampment on Loudoun Heights.

Browne, Dunn. *Mr. Dunn Browne's Experiences in the Army*. Boston: Nichols and Noyes, 1866. Insightful perspectives on the miseries of army life during the fall occupation following Antietam.

Frye, Dennis E. *Antietam Revealed*. Collingswood, New Jersey: Civil War Historicals, 2004. Includes summary chapters on the Confederate invasion of Maryland, the Battle of Harpers Ferry, and the debate between General McClellan and the War Department over the fortification of Harpers Ferry.

——————. "Drama Between the Rivers." *Antietam: Essays on the 1862 Maryland Campaign*. Gary W. Gallagher, ed. Kent State University Press: 1989. Concise narrative of the largest battle at Harpers Ferry.

——————. "Stonewall Attacks: The Siege of Harpers Ferry." *Blue & Gray Magazine*. Vol. 5, Issue 1, August–September 1987. Detailed account of the largest combat action at Harpers Ferry during the war.

Goddard, A. A. *Portland Daily Press*. Mrs. Goddard contributed articles describing life as a matron for the Clayton General Hospital during the summer to her hometown newspaper in Portland, Maine.

Gould, John M. *History of the First, Tenth, Twenty-Ninth Maine Regiment*. Portland: Stephen Berry, 1871. Highlights Dixon Miles and Railroad Brigade and occupation post-Antietam.

Harwood, Herbert H., Jr. *Impossible Challenge: The Baltimore & Ohio Railroad in Maryland*. Baltimore: Barnard, Roberts and Company, Inc., 1979. Includes the diary entries of Master of the Road John L. Wilson that chronicles the repeated destruction and reconstruction of the railroad bridge.

Jordan, William B., Jr. *The Civil War Journals of John Meade Gould*. Baltimore: Butternut and Blue, 1997. Gould's unbridled observations of Union occupation in early spring and return following Antietam.

Murfin, James V. *The Gleam of Bayonets: The Battle of Antietam and Robert E. Lee's Maryland Campaign, September 1862*. New York: A. S. Barnes and Company, 1964. Includes good chapters on the siege and capture of Harpers Ferry and the escape of the Union cavalry.

Raus, Edmund J. *Ministering Angel: The Reminiscences of Harriet A. Dada, a Union Army Nurse in the Civil War*. Gettysburg: Thomas Publications, 2004. Nurse Dada's vivid account while working at the Island Hospital.

Schildt, John W. *Four Days in October*. Private Printing, 1978. Succinct account of Lincoln's visit to the army following the Antietam Campaign.

Sears, Stephen W., ed. *The Civil War Papers of George B. McClellan: Selected Correspondence, 1860–1865*. New York: Ticknor and Fields, 1989. Includes McClellan's perspectives on the strategic value of Harpers Ferry in the spring and following the Antietam Campaign.

Quaife, Milo M., ed. *From the Cannon's Mouth: The Civil War Letters of Alpheus S. Williams*. Detroit: Wayne State University Press and the Detroit Historical Society, 1959. Perspective of the Union commander who occupied Maryland Heights following Antietam.

Walker, John G. "Jackson's Capture of Harper's Ferry." *Battles and Leaders of the Civil War*. Vol. 2. New York: The Century Company, 1887. A surviving Confederate general recalls the story.

White, Julius. "The Surrender of Harper's Ferry." *Battles and Leaders of the Civil War*. Vol. 2. New York: The Century Company, 1887. The perspective from the Union general who surrendered to Stonewall Jackson.

Wingate, George W. *History of the 22nd Regiment of the National Guard of the State of New York*. New York: Edwin W. Dayton, 1896. Best account of military life in Harpers Ferry during the summer of 1862. Includes outstanding array of campground photographs.

1863

Lincoln, William S. *Life with the 34th Massachusetts Infantry*. Worcester: Press of Noyes, Snow and Company, 1879. Journal of life in Harpers Ferry through the eyes of the regiment's lieutenant colonel.

1864

Drickamer, Lee and Karen, eds. *Fort Lyon to Harpers Ferry: On the Border of North and South with "Rambling Jour."* Shippensburg, Pennsylvania: White Mane Publishing Company, 1987. Detailed letters by a clerk in the provost marshal operations, featuring insights into martial law and day-to-day soldier life in Harpers Ferry.

Early, Jubal Anderson. *War Memoirs*. Indiana University Press, 1960. Commanding general's account of the Confederate advance against the Ferry and Maryland Heights fortifications during the last Confederate invasion of the North.

Frye, Dennis E. "I Resolved to Play a Bold Game: John S. Mosby as a Factor in the 1864 Valley Campaign." *Struggle for the Shenandoah: Essays on the 1864 Valley Campaign*. Gary W. Gallagher, ed. The Kent State University Press, 1991. Analysis of Mosby's strategy and tactics versus Sheridan's countermeasures to protect his logistics.

Marmion, Annie P. *Under Fire: An Experience in the Civil War*. Private Printing, 1959. Doleful account by a preteen resident throughout the war, with emphasis on the bombardment of 1864.

National Archives, Record Group 109, Prisoner Records, Box 131, Harpers Ferry, West Virginia. Unpublished listings of Confederate prisoners of war processed through Harpers Ferry.

Taylor, James E. *The James E. Taylor Sketchbook: With Sheridan Up the Shenandoah Valley in 1864*. Dayton, Ohio: Morningside House, Inc., 1989. Dramatic first-hand account and illustrations of Harpers Ferry during Sheridan's famous campaign.

Tulane University, American Missionary Association Documents: 1864–1869. Unpublished letters and day-school reports of W. W. Wheeler and Ellen P. T. Wheeler for May–July 1864. Dramatic insights into the earliest known wartime school established to educate former slaves.

Index

About the Author

Dennis E. Frye is the Chief Historian at Harpers Ferry National Historical Park. Writer, lecturer, guide, and preservationist, Dennis is a prominent Civil War historian. Dennis has made numerous appearances on PBS, The History Channel, The Discovery Channel, and A&E as a guest historian, and he helped produce award-winning television features on the Battle of Antietam and abolitionist John Brown. As an associate producer for the Civil War movie *Gods and Generals*, Dennis recruited and coordinated nearly 3,000 re-enactors for the film.

One of the nation's leading Civil War battlefield preservationists, Dennis is co-founder and first president of the Save Historic Antietam Foundation, and he is co-founder and a former president of today's Civil War Trust, where he helped save battlefields in twelve states. Dennis is a tour guide in demand, leading tours for organizations such as the Smithsonian, National Geographic, numerous colleges and universities, and Civil War Round Tables.

A well-known author, Dennis has written 77 articles and six books. His latest book is entitled *Antietam Revealed*. He is currently writing a book entitled *September Suspense: Lincoln's Union in Peril*, which will detail the first invasion of the North and the Maryland Campaign. His articles have appeared in prestigious Civil War magazines such as *Civil War Times Illustrated*, *America's Civil War*, *Blue & Gray Magazine*, *North and South Magazine*, and *Hallowed Ground*, and he has been a guest contributor to the *Washington Post*.

Dennis resides near the Antietam Battlefield in Maryland, and he and his wife Sylvia have restored the home that was used by General Ambrose Burnside as his post-Antietam headquarters.